Celebrating Sunday for Catholic Families
2020–2021

Karla Hardersen

LTP

LITURGY
TRAINING
PUBLICATIONS

Nihil Obstat
Rev. Mr. Daniel G. Welter, JD
Chancellor
Archdiocese of Chicago
August 26, 2019

Imprimatur
Most Rev. Ronald A. Hicks
Vicar General
Archdiocese of Chicago
August 26, 2019

The *Nihil Obstat* and *Imprimatur* are declarations that the material is free from doctrinal or moral error, and thus is granted permission to publish in accordance with c. 827. No legal responsibility is assumed by the grant of this permission. No implication is contained herein that those who have granted the *Nihil Obstat* and *Imprimatur* agree with the content, opinions, or statements expressed.

CELEBRATING SUNDAY FOR CATHOLIC FAMILIES 2020–2021 © 2020 Archdiocese of Chicago: Liturgy Training Publications, 3949 South Racine Avenue, Chicago, IL 60609; 800-933-1800; fax: 800-933-7094; email: orders@ltp.org; website: www.LTP.org. All rights reserved.

This book was edited by Michaela I. Tudela. Christian Rocha was the production editor, Anna Manhart was the designer, and Kari Nicholls was the production artist.

Cover art © William Hernandez.

Printed in the United States of America

ISBN 978-1-61671-540-3

CSCF21

"You shall love the LORD your God with all your heart, and with all your soul, and with all your might. Keep these words that I am commanding to you today in your heart. Recite them to your children and talk about them when you are at home and when you are away, when you lie down and when you rise."

(Deuteronomy 6:5–7)

Contents

How to Use

Celebrating Sunday
for Catholic Families

This small weekly guide draws on the Gospel for each Sunday
and Holyday for the coming year. It is intended to help parents
engage their children with the Mass and deepen their appre-
ciation of the richness of their faith life. Very often, going to
Mass becomes a weekly event that begins and ends at the church
door. The brief reflection on an excerpt from the Gospel is
intended to spark your thinking about the Scripture that will
lead to conversation with your family before and after Mass.
Suggestions for questions and conversation starters are provided,
as well as some practice or practical way to carry this reflection
into the life of the family. Keep in mind, however, that sometimes you may have other needs, concerns, or ideas that are
more relevant to your home life at that moment. If so, engage
your children with those.

Note that very young children are able to enter into the liturgy
through their senses. Singing the hymns, calling their attention
to the changing colors of the liturgical seasons, and sitting
where they can observe the gestures of the Mass are all ways
to form them in the faith. Always remember, as the rite of
Baptism proclaims, you, as parents, are your children's first
and most important teachers. We hope that this book will
enrich your family's life of faith.

September 6, 2020

Twenty-Third Sunday in Ordinary Time

Hearing the Word
Matthew 18:15–20

In the name of the Father, and of the Son, and of the Holy Spirit.

Jesus said to his disciples: "If your brother sins against you, go and tell him his fault between you and him alone. If he listens to you, you have won over your brother. If he does not listen, take one or two others along with you, so that 'every fact may be established on the testimony of two or three witnesses.' If he refuses to listen to them, tell the church. If he refuses to listen even to the church, then treat him as you would a Gentile or a tax collector. Amen, I say to you, whatever you bind on earth shall be bound in heaven, and whatever you loose on earth shall be loosed in heaven. Again, amen, I say to you, if two of you agree on earth about anything for which they are to pray, it shall be granted to them by my heavenly Father. For where two or three are gathered together in my name, there am I in the midst of them."

Reflecting on the Word

Often when we are wronged, we complain about it to someone else or we let the disagreement fester in our hearts. Each reaction is harmful to ourselves, the other person, and the community. In this Gospel reading, Jesus is telling us to do the opposite: talk to the person who has wronged us directly. If that doesn't work, ask first for another member of your community to confront that person with you, and then bring it to the whole community to moderate. Jesus tells us that he is present when we are seeking reconciliation and praying together as a community.

•••••• ON THE WAY TO MASS

Is there a misunderstanding or argument with someone that is weighing heavily on your heart?

ON THE WAY HOME FROM MASS ••••••

How can you listen to someone even if that person wronged you?

Living the Word

With your children, compile a list of qualities that are needed to listen to someone (for example, patience, empathy, eye contact, focus, and so on). Practice listening to one another throughout the week. Each night, recall and identify which qualities were used to listen well. Discuss whether it is easier to listen when you are friendly or angry. Model arguments in which each child can practice being the wronged party by confronting the one who has hurt them. Talk about how they can use this to initiate moments of reconciliation.

September 13, 2020

Twenty-Fourth Sunday in Ordinary Time

Hearing the Word

Matthew 18:21–22

In the name of the Father, and of the Son, and of the Holy Spirit.

Peter approached Jesus and asked him, "Lord, if my brother sins against me, how often must I forgive? As many as seven times?" Jesus answered, "I say to you, not seven times but seventy-seven times."

Reflecting on the Word

Peter asked Jesus, "How often must I forgive?" Jesus responds very clearly, "I say to you, not seven times but seventy-seven times." This is a maxim, a simple phrase that is a code or rule of how to live as Jesus wants us to live. Here, Jesus is teaching us about radical forgiveness—that not only must we forgive, but also forgive fully and completely. Not an easy task for children or adults, especially when we experience suffering and betrayal. But Jesus teaches that God will forgive us, and wants us to forgive others, so that we might love as God loves us.

•••••• ON THE WAY TO MASS

When is the last time you forgave someone for hurting you? Have you recently asked for forgiveness?

ON THE WAY HOME FROM MASS ••••••

How many times does Jesus say we must forgive someone? Does he mean that when we reach the number 77 we can stop forgiving?

Living the Word

On construction paper or card stock, write Jesus' maxim clearly in the center: "I say to you, not seven times but seventy-seven times." Invite your children to decorate around the maxim. Hang these prominently near their bed or display them on their nightstand or tape them on the wall. Each night, discuss their day: Did they forgive anyone? Did they ask Jesus for forgiveness? How do they feel after forgiving someone? How does it feel to know that Jesus forgives them?

September 20, 2020

Twenty-Fifth Sunday in Ordinary Time

Hearing the Word
Matthew 20:8–15

In the name of the Father, and of the Son, and of the Holy Spirit.

"When it was evening, the owner of the vineyard said to his foreman, 'Summon the laborers and give them their pay, beginning with the last and ending with the first.' When those who had started about five o'clock came, each received the usual daily wage. So when the first came, they thought that they would receive more, but each of them also got the usual wage. And on receiving it they grumbled against the land-owner, saying, 'These last ones worked only one hour, and you have made them equal to us, who bore the day's burden and the heat.' He said to one of them in reply, 'My friend, I am not cheating you. Did you not agree with me for the usual daily wage? Take what is yours and go. Are you envious because I am generous?'"

Reflecting on the Word

In this parable, Jesus is comparing the Kingdom of heaven to a generous landowner who gives the same amount of pay to the workers who came at the end of the day as the workers who were there all day. Our understanding of fairness is in stark contrast to God's abounding generosity. Jesus reminds us that God gives love and grace freely to everyone.

•••••• ON THE WAY TO MASS

Have you ever felt jealous of someone for having more than you do? Have you ever felt that you have been treated unfairly?

ON THE WAY HOME FROM MASS ••••••

When have you ever received undeserved generosity?

Living the Word

Create a chore chart for the week. Explain that some days will have more jobs than others. If you have more than one child, alternate their heavy days of chores. Decide on a small reward for the completion of the work, making sure each child receives the same reward no matter the amount or duration of work.

Discuss how it makes each child feel to receive the same reward regardless of the work. If one does not have to work as hard, can we rejoice for that person? Or are we jealous? How can we be more generous with others? Sometime this week, make a list of how we can share our gifts, talents, and time with others.

September 27, 2020

Twenty-Sixth Sunday in Ordinary Time

Hearing the Word

Matthew 21:28–32

In the name of the Father, and of the Son, and of the Holy Spirit.

Jesus said to the chief priests and elders of the people: "What is your opinion? A man had two sons. He came to the first and said, 'Son, go out and work in the vineyard today.' He said in reply, 'I will not,' but afterwards changed his mind and went. The man came to the other son and gave the same order. He said in reply, 'Yes, sir,' but did not go. Which of the two did his father's will?" They answered, "The first." Jesus said to them, "Amen, I say to you, tax collectors and prostitutes are entering the kingdom of God before you. When John came to you in the way of righteousness, you did not believe him; but tax collectors and prostitutes did. Yet even when you saw that, you did not later change your minds and believe him."

Reflecting on the Word

Sometimes what we say and what we do are very different. Jesus makes a point about those who promised to follow their word but didn't, and those that do. If our initial response to something is not in accordance with God's will, we can always change our minds and turn back to God. There is humility in changing one's mind, and in returning to God after initially turning away. No matter what we have done, it is never too late to return to God.

• • • • • • ON THE WAY TO MASS

Did you ever agree to do something and then not do it? When you didn't follow through on what you promised, how did it make the other person feel?

ON THE WAY HOME FROM MASS • • • • • •

Do actions speak louder than words?

Living the Word

Sometimes we impulsively say things that are not aligned with God's will. Discuss as a family when you have each said things that you didn't mean. How did you feel when you acknowledged that you spoke too quickly and rashly? What did you do to turn back to Jesus? How might we more easily think of how Jesus wants us to act before we do and say things we don't mean? Think of ways to help one another focus on responding in a way that reflects God's will.

October 4, 2020

Twenty-Seventh Sunday in Ordinary Time

Hearing the Word
Matthew 21:33–35, 37, 39–41

In the name of the Father, and of the Son, and of the Holy Spirit.

"There was a landowner who planted a vineyard, put a hedge around it, dug a wine press in it, and built a tower. Then he leased it to tenants and went on a journey. When vintage time drew near, he sent his servants to the tenants to obtain his produce. But the tenants seized the servants and one they beat, another they killed, and a third they stoned. Finally, he sent his son to them, thinking, 'They will respect my son.' They seized him, threw him out of the vineyard, and killed him. What will the owner of the vineyard do to those tenants when he comes?" They answered him, "He will put those wretched men to a wretched death and lease his vineyard to other tenants who will give him the produce at the proper times."

Reflecting on the Word

In this parable, we see God as a landowner who first sent messengers, or prophets, and then his son, Jesus, to gather the bounty of the vineyard. Jesus and the prophets are treated so harshly by the tenants of the vineyard that the parable ends with the landowner killing the wicked tenants. Do we reject God's messengers? Perhaps we need to be more accepting and pay closer attention to the people who are doing God's work.

......ON THE WAY TO MASS

Have we ever hurt or harmed anyone with a look, a harsh word, or a bad thought?

ON THE WAY HOME FROM MASS ......

How might we better discern that someone is doing God's will? How may we be more receptive to God and his messengers?

Living the Word

Discuss today's Gospel with your children with an art project. Draw a vineyard with lush plants and happy farmers. Talk about what the farmers must do to create such a beautiful, thriving place.

Now draw the same scene, but with people instead of vines. How does God help us grow and thrive?

October 11, 2020

Twenty-Eighth Sunday in Ordinary Time

Hearing the Word

Matthew 22:1–10

In the name of the Father, and of the Son, and of the Holy Spirit.

Jesus again in reply spoke to the chief priests and elders of the people in parables, saying, "The kingdom of heaven may be likened to a king who gave a wedding feast for his son. He dispatched his servants to summon the invited guests to the feast, but they refused to come. A second time he sent other servants, saying, 'Tell those invited: "Behold, I have prepared my banquet, my calves and fattened cattle are killed, and everything is ready; come to the feast."' Some ignored the invitation and went away, one to his farm, another to his business. The rest laid hold of his servants, mistreated them, and killed them. The king was enraged and sent his troops, destroyed those murderers, and burned their city. Then he said to his servants, 'The feast is ready, but those who were invited were not worthy to come. Go out, therefore, into the main roads and invite to the feast whomever you find.' The servants went out into the streets and gathered all they found, bad and good alike, and the hall was filled with guests."

Reflecting on the Word

In this parable, God is presented as a king preparing a wedding feast for his son. Many were invited, but they all rejected the invitation, through indifference or hostility. The king then opened the banquet to everyone—good and bad alike. In the same way, God invites us all to the table, but some reject the invitation. Those who are alert, accepting, and prepared for God's Word are worthy of the offer of salvation.

•••••• ON THE WAY TO MASS

Has anyone ever declined your invitation? How did it make you feel?

ON THE WAY HOME FROM MASS ••••••

God is always inviting us to come to him. How do we respond to his invitation?

Living the Word

Together, make a list of all the ways you can be ready to prepare for God's presence in your life. How can your heart be ready? How can your mind be ready? How can your hands be ready?

This week, before bed, make a list of the ways God was active throughout the day. Did you talk to people with kindness? Did you try to think as Jesus would? Did you see the good in people? How does preparing for God's presence help you be more welcoming to the love of Jesus throughout your day?

October 18, 2020

Twenty-Ninth Sunday in Ordinary Time

Hearing the Word

Matthew 22:15–21

In the name of the Father, and of the Son, and of the Holy Spirit.

The Pharisees went off and plotted how they might entrap Jesus in speech. They sent their disciples to him, with the Herodians, saying, "Teacher, we know that you are a truthful man and that you teach the way of God in accordance with the truth. And you are not concerned with anyone's opinion, for you do not regard a person's status. Tell us, then, what is your opinion: Is it lawful to pay the census tax to Caesar or not?" Knowing their malice, Jesus said, "Why are you testing me, you hypocrites? Show me the coin that pays the census tax." Then they handed him the Roman coin. He said to them, "Whose image is this and whose inscription?" They replied, "Caesar's." At that he said to them, "Then repay to Caesar what belongs to Caesar and to God what belongs to God."

Reflecting on the Word

The Pharisees, scholars of Jewish law, were trying to trick Jesus into denouncing the rulers of his day. But Jesus refused to be tested and told them to give to Caesar what is Caesar's, and to God what is God's. There is a separation between the earthly realm and the realm of God. Although we are part of a society on earth and must pay our dues and taxes, the realm of God can intercept and weave through every aspect of our lives. We can acknowledge the primacy of God by doing God's work in all areas of our lives—not just during Mass and prayers, but by doing our daily work and living in a way that reflects God's will.

...... ON THE WAY TO MASS

What matters belong to humanity? What matters belong to God?

ON THE WAY HOME FROM MASS ......

Recall your responses to what belongs to humanity and what belongs to God. After hearing today's Gospel and homily, have your responses changed?

Living the Word

Explain that throughout history there have been clashes between the laws of humankind and the laws of God. But how might we, as Catholic Christians, live in the secular world and reflect our religious values?

October 25, 2020

Thirtieth Sunday in Ordinary Time

Hearing the Word

Matthew 22:36–40

In the name of the Father, and of the Son, and of the Holy Spirit.

"Teacher, which commandment in the law is the greatest?"
He said to him, "You shall love the Lord, your God, with all
your heart, with all your soul, and with all your mind. This is
the greatest and the first commandment. The second is like it:
You shall love your neighbor as yourself. The whole law and
the prophets depend on these two commandments."

Reflecting on the Word

In this reading, we can summarize the whole point of the Gospel: love. Jesus was asked what the greatest commandment was, and he gave two—love for God and love for neighbor. In 2014, Pope Francis said that because Jesus joined these two commandments together, "they are in fact inseparable and complementary. . . . You cannot love God without loving your neighbor, and you cannot love your neighbor without loving God" (*Angelus*).

•••••• ON THE WAY TO MASS

How do you define love?

ON THE WAY HOME FROM MASS ••••••

It is easy to love someone who loves you back. How might you love someone you don't know very well, or someone who doesn't like you?

Living the Word

Discuss with your children how they might show a neighbor how much they love them. This could be someone on your block, someone from your community, or someone you don't know very well. Write a list of your ideas: conversing, making a gift of food, helping with yardwork, and so on. Plan to do one of these things as a family. Afterward, talk about how these actions made your children feel. How is loving your neighbor like loving God? Determine as a family whether you can implement this as a weekly or monthly family activity.

November 1, 2020

Solemnity of All Saints

Hearing the Word
Matthew 5:3–12a

In the name of the Father, and of the Son, and of the Holy Spirit.

[Jesus said:] "Blessed are the poor in spirit, / for theirs is
the kingdom of heaven. / Blessed are they who mourn, /
for they will be comforted. / Blessed are the meek, / for they
will inherit the land. / Blessed are they who hunger and
thirst for righteousness, / for they will be satisfied. / Blessed
are the merciful, / for they will be shown mercy. / Blessed are
the clean of heart, / for they will see God. / Blessed are the
peacemakers, / for they will be called children of God. / Blessed
are they who are persecuted for the sake of righteousness, /
for theirs is the Kingdom of heaven. / Blessed are you when
they insult you and persecute you / and utter every kind of
evil against you [falsely] because of me. / Rejoice and be glad, /
for your reward will be great in heaven."

Reflecting on the Word

The Solemnity of All Saints is a celebration honoring all men and women who have followed in the footsteps of Jesus. The blessed, or happy, are those disciples who are simple and humble before God, those who mourn for others, those who are poor and hungry, those who forgive and show mercy, those who seek peace, those who fight for justice, and those who respond to evil and suffering with goodness. Jesus teaches that true happiness and joy comes in following this difficult road to discipleship.

······ ON THE WAY TO MASS

Do you think it's a blessing to mourn or to hunger or to be persecuted?

ON THE WAY HOME FROM MASS ······

Being Jesus' disciple is very hard, but the saints are wonderful examples that ordinary people can do it. Which Beatitude can we practice today?

Living the Word

During evening prayers, thank God for the gifts we receive (the people in our lives, God's love and mercy, our many blessings). Create a "thanksgiving" tree: cut out leaf shapes in fall colors. Each child should write what he or she is thankful for on a leaf. Place some branches in a vase and tie the leaves to the branch. Each day, add another leaf to your tree. Talk about how many blessings God has given, and how we should remind ourselves to be thankful for these gifts.

November 8, 2020

THIRTY-SECOND SUNDAY IN ORDINARY TIME

Hearing the Word

Matthew 25:1–13

In the name of the Father, and of the Son, and of the Holy Spirit.

Jesus told his disciples this parable: "The kingdom of heaven will be like ten virgins who took their lamps and went out to meet the bridegroom. Five of them were foolish and five were wise. The foolish ones, when taking their lamps, brought no oil with them, but the wise brought flasks of oil with their lamps. Since the bridegroom was long delayed, they all became drowsy and fell asleep. At midnight, there was a cry, 'Behold, the bridegroom! Come out to meet him!' Then all those virgins got up and trimmed their lamps. The foolish ones said to the wise, 'Give us some of your oil, for our lamps are going out.' But the wise ones replied, 'No, for there may not be enough for us and you. Go instead to the merchants and buy some for yourselves.' While they went off to buy it, the bridegroom came and those who were ready went into the wedding feast with him. Then the door was locked. Afterwards the other virgins came and said, 'Lord, Lord, open the door for us!' But he said in reply, 'Amen, I say to you, I do not know you.' Therefore, stay awake, for you know neither the day nor the hour."

Reflecting on the Word

In this parable, the door to the Kingdom of heaven is open to all who are prepared and ready to enter through it. The wise disciples of Jesus await his presence and acknowledge that their time is not God's time. They are prepared and ready to go at a moment's notice, while the foolish have not prepared themselves adequately. We have a responsibility for our own preparedness and need to be present to enter the Kingdom of heaven. We need to be awake, attentive, and fully available to walk through the door.

•••••• ON THE WAY TO MASS

What does it feel like to be unprepared?

ON THE WAY HOME FROM MASS ••••••

Why is it good to be prepared? What preparations must we make now to meet God someday?

Living the Word

We celebrate Thanksgiving in a couple of weeks. Before we feast, we need to prepare. Discuss as a family what is needed to be ready for Thanksgiving: grocery shopping, cooking and baking, decorating, or packing suitcases for traveling. Make a list. Ask the children which tasks they would like to help complete. Assist them as needed on their chosen assignments. Ask them how they would prepare if Jesus were coming to the celebration. How can they be ready for Jesus' presence at the table?

Thirty-Third Sunday in Ordinary Time

Hearing the Word
Matthew 25:14–15, 19–21

In the name of the Father, and of the Son, and of the Holy Spirit.

Jesus told his disciples this parable: "A man going on a journey called in his servants and entrusted his possessions to them. To one he gave five talents; to another, two; to a third, one—to each according to his ability. Then he went away.

"After a long time the master of those servants came back and settled accounts with them. The one who had received five talents came forward bringing the additional five. He said, 'Master, you gave me five talents. See, I have made five more.' His master said to him, 'Well done, my good and faithful servant. Since you were faithful in small matters, I will give you great responsibilities. Come, share your master's joy.'"

Reflecting on the Word

God expects that we use, cultivate, nourish, and expand the talents and gifts we have been given. We are asked to use and invest our talents fully for ourselves and for others, in God's name. When we do, our gifts are made more bountiful.

······ ON THE WAY TO MASS

What talents do you have?

ON THE WAY HOME FROM MASS ······

How does Jesus want us to use our talents?

Living the Word

Help your children identify gifts and talents that God has given them. These need not be what they are good at, such as playing a sport or being musically inclined or adding numbers up in their heads. What facets of their personalities shine? Does your child leaven situations with humor? Is he or she patient or a good listener? Help your children think of ways to use these gifts as a disciple of Jesus. How can you use these gifts to make the world a better place, both individually and as a family?

November 22, 2020

Solemnity of Our Lord Jesus Christ, King of the Universe

Hearing the Word

Matthew 25:31–34

In the name of the Father, and of the Son, and of the Holy Spirit.

Jesus said to his disciples: "When the Son of Man comes in his glory, and all the angels with him, he will sit upon his glorious throne, and all the nations will be assembled before him. And he will separate them one from another, as a shepherd separates the sheep from the goats. He will place the sheep on his right and the goats on his left. Then the king will say to those on his right, 'Come, you who are blessed by my Father. Inherit the kingdom prepared for you from the foundation of the world.'"

Reflecting on the Word

As we end our liturgical year and enter a new season, Advent, we deepen our image and understanding of Jesus Christ as the King of the Universe. Jesus is both a king sitting on his throne before all the nations and a shepherd separating the good sheep from the bad. This imagery of a judgment leads us to ask by which measure we will be judged. As Jesus told us a few weeks ago, the greatest commandments are the love of God and the love of neighbor. How have we ministered to or failed to minister to God and neighbor? Jesus as King and Good Shepherd wants to rule over our lives and hearts in the works of love, justice, and mercy.

• • • • • • ON THE WAY TO MASS

What is the role of a king? How does a human king differ from Christ the King?

ON THE WAY HOME FROM MASS • • • • • •

How could we help bring about love, justice, and mercy into our lives?

Living the Word

Have your children create a crown and decorate it ornately. Announce that every day this week, one member of the family will be king or queen for the day. Discuss what are the job responsibilities for the king or queen, such as determining the chores, schedule, meals for the day, and so on. Then discuss how Jesus rules. How can the day's ruler also imitate Jesus and bring love, justice, and mercy into the day?

November 29, 2020

First Sunday of Advent

Hearing the Word
Mark 13:33–37

In the name of the Father, and of the Son, and of the Holy Spirit.

Jesus said to his disciples: "Be watchful! Be alert! You do not know when the time will come. It is like a man traveling abroad. He leaves home and places his servants in charge, each with his own work, and orders the gatekeeper to be on the watch. Watch, therefore; you do not know when the lord of the house is coming, whether in the evening, or at midnight, or at cockcrow, or in the morning. May he not come suddenly and find you sleeping. What I say to you, I say to all: 'Watch!'"

Reflecting on the Word

Today we begin a new liturgical season and year. We also begin a time of waiting for the birth of Jesus. Waiting always involves patience and expectation. But in this Gospel, Jesus reminds us that we also must be prepared, watchful, and alert. We must be vigilant and attentive in our waiting—hard to do amidst the distractions of the commerce of Christmas. In Advent, we must focus on Jesus.

• • • • • • ON THE WAY TO MASS

Have you ever waited for someone to visit? What did you do while you waited?

ON THE WAY HOME FROM MASS • • • • • •

What changes did you notice in the church environment? How do we prepare our home for the birth of Jesus?

Living the Word

Write down ideas of how your family can actively prepare for Jesus' coming. Write your ideas on little slips of paper and fold them in half. Ideas include singing Advent hymns such as "O Come, O Come, Emmanuel," making meals or baking cookies for someone in need, or setting up a nativity scene. Invite your children to participate in these activities each day during Advent. How does each activity make you ready for Jesus? Don't forget to set up an Advent wreath with four candles. Light a candle for each passing Sunday; explain that the brighter the wreath grows, the closer Jesus' arrival is.

December 6, 2020

Second Sunday of Advent

Hearing the Word

Mark 1:1–5, 7–8

In the name of the Father, and of the Son, and of the Holy Spirit.

The beginning of the gospel of Jesus Christ the Son of God.

As it is written in Isaiah the prophet: / *Behold, I am sending my messenger ahead of you; / he will prepare your way. / A voice of one crying out in the desert: / "Prepare the way of the Lord, / make straight his paths." /* John the Baptist appeared in the desert proclaiming a baptism of repentance for the forgiveness of sins. People of the whole Judean countryside and all the inhabitants of Jerusalem were going out to him and were being baptized by him in the Jordan River as they acknowledged their sins. And this is what he proclaimed: "One mightier than I is coming after me. I am not worthy to stoop and loosen the thongs of his sandals. I have baptized you with water; he will baptize you with the Holy Spirit."

Reflecting on the Word

In the very first verse of his Gospel, Mark identifies Jesus as not just the Son of David, the Messiah, whom the Jewish people were long awaiting, but *the Son of God.* We are then introduced to John the Baptist, who prepares the way for the Son of God by preaching repentance and forgiveness of sins. To sin is to separate or alienate oneself from God. John offered baptism to those who repented their sins before God and readied themselves to receive God's forgiveness, while acknowledging that one is coming who can baptize them not just with water, but with the Holy Spirit.

......ON THE WAY TO MASS

At Mass, we will hear John the Baptist preparing the way of the Lord. Listen closely to what he says we need to do.

ON THE WAY HOME FROM MASS ......

How can we ready our spirits for the Son of God this Advent?

Living the Word

On this Second Sunday of Advent, add a visual representation of the Holy Spirit to your family's nativity. Use red and orange tissue paper to decorate a glass votive (a mason or jelly jar will do) and light a votive candle inside. Or draw and cut out doves to fly over the manger. Pray together for the Holy Spirit to come and fill your hearts.

Solemnity of the Immaculate Conception of the Blessed Virgin Mary

Hearing the Word

Luke 1:26–38

In the name of the Father, and of the Son, and of the Holy Spirit.

The angel Gabriel was sent from God to a town of Galilee called Nazareth, to a virgin betrothed to a man named Joseph, of the house of David, and the virgin's name was Mary. And coming to her, he said, "Hail, full of grace! The Lord is with you." But she was greatly troubled at what was said and pondered what sort of greeting this might be. Then the angel said to her, "Do not be afraid, Mary, for you have found favor with God. Behold, you will conceive in your womb and bear a son, and you shall name him Jesus. He will be great and will be called Son of the Most High, and the Lord God will give him the throne of David his father, and he will rule over the house of Jacob forever, and of his Kingdom there will be no end." But Mary said to the angel, "How can this be, since I have no relations with a man?" And the angel said to her in reply, "The Holy Spirit will come upon you, and the power of the Most High will overshadow you. Therefore the child to be born will be called holy, the Son of God. And behold, Elizabeth, your relative, has also conceived a son in her old age, and this is the sixth month for her who was called barren; for nothing will be impossible for God." Mary said, "Behold, I am the handmaid of the Lord. May it be done to me according to your word." Then the angel departed from her.

Reflecting on the Word

Even though Mary lived in a world that was fraught with sin, she was not touched by it. God filled her with so much grace and mercy. When told that she would carry the Son of the Most High, she said yes to God without condition. Her yes changed her life—and ours.

......ON THE WAY TO MASS

Have you ever said no to someone and later regretted it? How did that make you feel?

ON THE WAY HOME FROM MASS ......

When was the last time you said yes to God?

Living the Word

Ask your children why they might respond no sometimes. Talk about how Mary might have felt when the angel Gabriel approached her with good news. Talk about how she felt "greatly troubled." She might have felt a mixture of surprise, nervousness, confusion. But in the end, she said yes. She had great faith and trust in God and the goodness he had shown to her. This week, ask your children to think of one thing they would normally say no to and to say yes—without fear, without hesitation, full of trust in God.

December 13, 2020

Third Sunday of Advent

Hearing the Word

John 1:6–8, 23–28

In the name of the Father, and of the Son, and of the Holy Spirit.

A man named John was sent from God. He came for testimony, to testify to the light, so that all might believe through him. He was not the light, but came to testify to the light.

[John] said: / "I am *the voice of one crying in the desert,* / *'Make straight the way of the Lord,'* / as Isaiah the prophet said." Some Pharisees were also sent. They asked him, "Why, then, do you baptize if you are not the Christ or Elijah or the Prophet?" John answered them, "I baptize with water; but there is one among you whom you do not recognize, the one who is coming after me, whose sandal strap I am not worthy to untie." This happened in Bethany across the Jordan where John was baptizing.

Reflecting on the Word

Today is Gaudete Sunday. We are so close to the birth of Jesus, we begin to rejoice! We light the rose-colored candle on the Advent wreath, reminding us of that joy. Once again, we encounter John the Baptist, who acknowledged that he is not the light (the Messiah), but that he came to testify to the light so that many would believe through him. We are also called to reflect the light of Christ by our words and actions. Though we are unworthy, as John was, we are called to be light to each other in all that we say and do.

• • • • • • ON THE WAY TO MASS

Christmas is coming closer. Ask your family to observe what signs at Mass tell us that Christmas is near.

ON THE WAY HOME FROM MASS • • • • • •

Why is Jesus described as "the light"?

Living the Word

Help your children carefully and safely place a lit candle in front of a mirror. Notice and discuss the differences between the actual light and the light in the reflection. Write a list of Jesus' qualities and actions. Then make a list of how you could reflect those same qualities and imitate those actions. Near the end of the week, have your children draw a side profile of themselves facing Jesus. How can we reflect and follow Jesus in our lives?

Fourth Sunday of Advent

Hearing the Word
Luke 1:31–38

In the name of the Father, and of the Son, and of the Holy Spirit.

[The angel said, to Mary,] "Behold, you will conceive in your womb and bear a son, and you shall name him Jesus. He will be great and will be called Son of the Most High, and the Lord God will give him the throne of David his father, and he will rule over the house of Jacob forever, and of his kingdom there will be no end." But Mary said to the angel, "How can this be, since I have no relations with a man?" And the angel said to her in reply, "The Holy Spirit will come upon you, and the power of the Most High will overshadow you. Therefore the child to be born will be called holy, the Son of God. And behold, Elizabeth, your relative, has also conceived a son in her old age, and this is the sixth month for her who was called barren; for nothing will be impossible for God." Mary said, "Behold, I am the handmaid of the Lord. May it be done to me according to your word." Then the angel departed from her.

Reflecting on the Word

Mary was chosen to bear the Messiah. Through her, God was able to be fully with us in our humanity. She committed herself to following God's plan for her, though she did not understand it. Mary reminds us to allow ourselves to be loved, and to be transformed by that love so that we can follow God in all we do and say, all the days of our lives.

• • • • • • ON THE WAY TO MASS

How does it make you feel that God loved us so much he sent his Son to be with us?

ON THE WAY HOME FROM MASS • • • • • •

God gave us the gift of Jesus. How does it show how much God loves us? How can we share that love with others?

Living the Word

The angel Gabriel brought Mary a message of God's love. As Christmas is only a few days away, spend time making homemade cards for those close to you. Gather art supplies and enlist your children to personalize each greeting. Include messages of love and joy.

December 25, 2020

SOLEMNITY OF THE NATIVITY OF THE LORD (MASS AT NIGHT)

Hearing the Word

Luke 2:1–7a, 8–14

In the name of the Father, and of the Son, and of the Holy Spirit.

In those days a decree went out from Caesar Augustus that the whole world should be enrolled. This was the first enrollment, when Quirinius was governor of Syria. So all went to be enrolled, each to his own town. And Joseph too went up from Galilee from the town of Nazareth to Judea, to the city of David that is called Bethlehem, because he was of the house and family of David, to be enrolled with Mary, his betrothed, who was with child. While they were there, the time came for her to have her child, and she gave birth to her firstborn son.

Now there were shepherds in that region living in the fields and keeping the night watch over their flock. The angel of the Lord appeared to them and the glory of the Lord shone around them, and they were struck with great fear. The angel said to them, "Do not be afraid; for behold, I proclaim to you good news of great joy that will be for all the people. For today in the city of David a savior has been born for you who is Christ and Lord. And this will be a sign for you: you will find an infant wrapped in swaddling clothes and lying in a manger." And suddenly there was a multitude of the

heavenly host with the angel, praising God and saying: /
"Glory to God in the highest / and on earth peace to those
on whom his favor rests."

Reflecting on the Word

Our wait is over! Jesus is born! We celebrate today and share
tidings of great joy. God has become the Word incarnate.
Jesus was born fully human to experience humanity so that
we might bear witness to his actions, words, and life and
thereby follow his example. As we celebrate our Savior's
birth today, may our hearts be filled with great joy, wonder,
and awe!

•••••• ON THE WAY TO MASS

Jesus was born a baby, just like you were. What are your thoughts
that God came to be like one of us?

ON THE WAY HOME FROM MASS ••••••

The angels rejoiced in the heavens that Jesus was born. How
would you share the Good News with others?

Living the Word

Find small bells to attach to a length of wide ribbon. During
your family meal, during prayer time, or perhaps before
opening gifts beneath the Christmas tree, sing like the
angels, ring your bells, and share the good news: "Glory to
God in the highest, and peace to God's people on earth!"
How does Jesus' birth fill you with joy?

December 27, 2020

Feast of the Holy Family of Jesus, Mary, and Joseph

Hearing the Word

Luke 2:22, 39–40

In the name of the Father, and of the Son, and of the Holy Spirit.

When the days were completed for their purification according to the law of Moses, they took him up to Jerusalem to present him to the Lord.

When they had fulfilled all the prescriptions of the law of the Lord, they returned to Galilee, to their own town of Nazareth. The child grew and became strong, filled with wisdom; and the favor of God was upon him.

Reflecting on the Word

The observance of Jewish rituals and customs were important to Mary and Joseph and were outward signs of their devotion to God. Though we know very little of Jesus' early years, we can imagine that his parents' love of God and trust in him bonded the family tightly together. We know Jesus grew and become strong, filled with knowledge and the grace of God.

• • • • • • ON THE WAY TO MASS

What traditions do we observe in our family? What religious rituals and customs are important to us?

ON THE WAY HOME FROM MASS • • • • • •

Why is going to Mass important?

Living the Word

Have your children draw and color a picture of the Holy Family. Imagine the family activities they must have done together and what they talked about. On another day, have your children draw a picture of your family. Talk about what your family does together, and what you frequently talk about when you are together. How are both families the same? How are they different? How might you become closer as a family? Place both pictures in a place of prominence in your home to review and reflect on throughout the week.

January 1, 2021

Solemnity of Mary, the Holy Mother of God

Hearing the Word

Luke 2:16–21

In the name of the Father, and of the Son, and of the Holy Spirit.

The shepherds went in haste to Bethlehem and found Mary and Joseph, and the infant lying in the manger. When they saw this, they made known the message that had been told them about this child. All who heard it were amazed by what had been told them by the shepherds. And Mary kept all these things, reflecting on them in her heart. Then the shepherds returned, glorifying and praising God for all they had heard and seen, just as it had been told to them.

When eight days were completed for his circumcision, he was named Jesus, the name given him by the angel before he was conceived in the womb.

Reflecting on the Word

After arriving in Bethlehem, the shepherds told their story about the angels appearing to them, proclaiming Jesus' birth. Everyone was amazed at what they heard. But Mary must have contemplated what her son's future would hold, much like most parents today. She knew that Jesus was already destined to be our Savior. His name and path in life were already predetermined by God.

......ON THE WAY TO MASS

Explain to your children that in the Gospel, they will hear that Jesus' name was given to Mary and Joseph before he was born. Tell your children why you gave them their name. Ask your children for their thoughts on their names.

ON THE WAY HOME FROM MASS ......

Do you have any concerns about the future of your children? Do any of them have any fears or worries about the future?

Living the Word

Gather craft supplies, including construction paper, crayons or markers, and decorative items. Have your children write their names boldly in block letters across the paper. Around the letters, they may write words that describe themselves, such as "loving," "kind," "sweet," "athletic," "artistic," and so on. Display their artwork. Ask your children how it feels to know that their parents and God specially chose their names.

January 3, 2021

Solemnity of the Epiphany of the Lord

Hearing the Word

Matthew 2:1–5, 7–11

In the name of the Father, and of the Son, and of the Holy Spirit.

When Jesus was born in Bethlehem of Judea, in the days of King Herod, behold, magi from the east arrived in Jerusalem, saying, "Where is the newborn king of the Jews? We saw his star at its rising and have come to do him homage." When King Herod heard this, he was greatly troubled, and all Jerusalem with him. Assembling all the chief priests and the scribes of the people, he inquired of them where the Messiah was to be born. They said to him, "In Bethlehem of Judea." Then Herod called the magi secretly and ascertained from them the time of the star's appearance. He sent them to Bethlehem and said, "Go and search diligently for the child. When you have found him, bring me word, that I too may go and do him homage." After their audience with the king they set out. And behold, the star that they had seen at its rising preceded them, until it came and stopped over the place where the child was. They were overjoyed at seeing the star, and on entering the house they saw the child with Mary his mother. They prostrated themselves and did him homage. Then they opened their treasures and offered him gifts of gold, frankincense, and myrrh.

Reflecting on the Word

Epiphany is the feast of manifestation, in which Jesus is revealed to be the Messiah, the Son of God. Jesus did not come to earth just for the Jews; rather, he welcomed all and came to heal the entire world. The Magi treated Jesus as they would a king. The star that led the Magi to Jesus is another symbol that identifies Jesus as the Light of the World.

•••••• ON THE WAY TO MASS

Today we are celebrating the Solemnity of the Epiphany of the Lord. What does the word *epiphany* mean?

ON THE WAY HOME FROM MASS ••••••

What gifts might we give to Jesus as this new year begins?

Living the Word

For centuries, many communities and families have blessed the entrances and doors to their homes and churches with chalk. As a family, bless the entrance to your home. You can find a blessing at http://www.usccb.org/prayer-and-worship/sacraments-and-sacramentals/sacramentals-blessings/ objects/blessing-of-the-home-and-household-on-epiphany.cfm.

Process to your front entrance, carrying lights (either candles or battery-powered lights), and singing "We Three Kings." Using chalk, write 20+C+M+B+21 on top of the door frame. The 20 and 21 symbolize the year, the + represents the cross, and the letters mark the three Magi—Caspar, Melchior, and Balthazar. This blessing is an outward sign and reminder that Christ may dwell in the home throughout the year.

Feast of the Baptism of the Lord

Hearing the Word

Mark 1:7–11

In the name of the Father, and of the Son, and of the Holy Spirit.

This is what John the Baptist proclaimed: "One mightier than I is coming after me. I am not worthy to stoop and loosen the thongs of his sandals. I have baptized you with water; he will baptize you with the Holy Spirit."

It happened in those days that Jesus came from Nazareth of Galilee and was baptized in the Jordan by John. On coming up out of the water he saw the heavens being torn open and the Spirit, like a dove, descending upon him. And a voice came from the heavens, "You are my beloved Son; with you I am well pleased."

Reflecting on the Word

All four Gospel narratives include the baptism of Jesus, attesting to its importance in his life and the beginning of his ministry. Jesus' baptism became the model of a sacrament of initiation, in which we are all welcomed in the Church and invited into our role as part of the Kingdom of God. God calls Jesus his Son, expresses love, and calls him by name. In our own Baptism, we are also recognized as a beloved child of God, and we are called by name into God's Kingdom.

•••••• ON THE WAY TO MASS

Explain to your children that they will hear about Jesus' baptism in today's Gospel. Ask them to recall Baptisms they have attended. What similarities and differences between those Baptisms and Jesus' can they name?

ON THE WAY HOME FROM MASS ••••••

Follow up on the question above. Then share memories of your children's Baptism.

Living the Word

Do you have photos or video of your children's Baptisms? Share them with your children. Who was there celebrating with you? What did your children wear? How did you feel on their baptismal day? Talk about the significance of holy water, of sacred oils, of the white baptismal garment. You might visit http://www.usccb.org/prayer-and-worship /sacraments-and-sacramentals/baptism/index.cfm and look at the resources listed.

January 17, 2021

Second Sunday in Ordinary Time

Hearing the Word

John 1:35–42

In the name of the Father, and of the Son, and of the Holy Spirit.

John was standing with two of his disciples, and as he watched Jesus walk by, he said, "Behold, the Lamb of God." The two disciples heard what he said and followed Jesus. Jesus turned and saw them following him and said to them, "What are you looking for?" They said to him, "Rabbi"—which translated means Teacher—, "where are you staying?" He said to them, "Come, and you will see." So they went and saw where he was staying, and they stayed with him that day. It was about four in the afternoon. Andrew, the brother of Simon Peter, was one of the two who heard John and followed Jesus. He first found his own brother Simon and told him, "We have found the Messiah"—which is translated Christ. Then he brought him to Jesus. Jesus looked at him and said, "You are Simon the son of John; you will be called Cephas"—which is translated Peter.

Reflecting on the Word

As we return to Ordinary Time, we learn more about Jesus and hear stories about his ministry. It is in this "ordinary time" we see Jesus as fully human: living, sleeping, eating, teaching, and working with his disciples. Yet even in the ordinary, those around Jesus recognize his extraordinariness. In this passage, we hear Jesus being called by many different names: Lamb of God, Rabbi, and Messiah—all wonderful titles that call to mind his divinity as well as his humanity. Which names of Jesus speak to our hearts as we pray and attempt to follow him? Is he the Lamb of God who takes away our sins? Is he the Teacher to whom we listen? Is he the Messiah, the Son of God that we adore?

······ ON THE WAY TO MASS

What are your favorite names for Jesus?

ON THE WAY HOME FROM MASS ······

How did the church change from Christmas Time to Ordinary Time? What colors did you notice in church today?

Living the Word

Together, think of names for Jesus, including the ones you heard in the Gospel. Compile a list of these names (Friend, Teacher, Christ, Lord, Light, and so on). Which is your favorite? How do these names help us know Jesus better?

Third Sunday in Ordinary Time

Hearing the Word
Mark 1:14–20

In the name of the Father, and of the Son, and of the Holy Spirit.

After John had been arrested, Jesus came to Galilee proclaiming the gospel of God: "This is the time of fulfillment. The kingdom of God is at hand. Repent, and believe in the gospel."

As he passed by the Sea of Galilee, he saw Simon and his brother Andrew casting their nets into the sea; they were fishermen. Jesus said to them, "Come after me, and I will make you fishers of men." Then they abandoned their nets and followed him. He walked along a little farther and saw James, the son of Zebedee, and his brother John. They too were in a boat mending their nets. Then he called them. So they left their father Zebedee in the boat along with the hired men and followed him.

Reflecting on the Word

Jesus begins his ministry in Galilee by proclaiming to all: "Repent and believe in the Gospel." He calls us to pay attention, to listen, and to believe what Jesus is saying. He calls us all to repent—to change how we think, what we believe, and how we live. He calls for a renewal of our minds and hearts to follow him. These four fishermen left their entire lives behind to become Jesus' disciples. How might we "catch" people and help them to follow Jesus? How can we change how we think and live in order to follow Jesus?

......ON THE WAY TO MASS

What are fishermen? What do they do?

ON THE WAY HOME FROM MASS ......

What does it mean to be a fisher of people?

Living the Word

Help your children draw fish shapes on construction paper and cut them out. On each fish shape, write one simple way that your family can better follow the Gospel (read the Bible together, pray, participate in a parish service project, and so on). Attach a paperclip to each fish. Make a fishing pole using a yardstick and attach a length of string and a magnet to one end.

This week, have your children "fish" for a way to live out the message of this Gospel. Scatter the fish upside-down and each day catch one of them. Then do that activity together.

January 31, 2021

Fourth Sunday in Ordinary Time

Hearing the Word

Mark 1:21–28

In the name of the Father, and of the Son, and of the Holy Spirit.

Then they came to Capernaum, and on the sabbath Jesus entered the synagogue and taught. The people were astonished at his teaching, for he taught them as one having authority and not as the scribes. In their synagogue was a man with an unclean spirit; he cried out, "What have you to do with us, Jesus of Nazareth? Have you come to destroy us? I know who you are—the Holy One of God!" Jesus rebuked him and said, "Quiet! Come out of him!" The unclean spirit convulsed him and with a loud cry came out of him. All were amazed and asked one another, "What is this? A new teaching with authority. He commands even the unclean spirits and they obey him." His fame spread everywhere throughout the whole region of Galilee.

Reflecting on the Word

In this Gospel, Jesus' command and conviction in both his teaching and deeds were so powerful that witnesses were amazed and astonished. This dramatic reading gives us a glimpse into the charismatic person that Jesus was. Do we have a similar response to Jesus' words and deeds?

······ ON THE WAY TO MASS

Have you ever been amazed at something you heard or saw? Why did you react with amazement?

ON THE WAY HOME FROM MASS ······

What do you think of today's Gospel? Are we amazed, astonished, overwhelmed, and full of wonder and awe of Jesus?

Living the Word

Explain to your children that bad feelings, such as anger or jealousy, make our spirits "unclean." Make a list with your children of all the ways they might be separated from God lately—that is, when they've been mad at someone, when they've hurt someone, when they don't feel loved, when they forget to pray, and so on. Talk about how these things stand between us and God. How might we keep our heart and mind ready and accepting of God's love and presence? If your children have already received the Sacrament of Reconciliation, plan to go to confession as a family.

February 7, 2021

Fifth Sunday in Ordinary Time

Hearing the Word

Mark 1:29–39

In the name of the Father, and of the Son, and of the Holy Spirit.

On leaving the synagogue Jesus entered the house of Simon and Andrew with James and John. Simon's mother-in-law lay sick with a fever. They immediately told him about her. He approached, grasped her hand, and helped her up. Then the fever left her and she waited on them.

When it was evening, after sunset, they brought to him all who were ill or possessed by demons. The whole town was gathered at the door. He cured many who were sick with various diseases, and he drove out many demons, not permitting them to speak because they knew him.

Rising very early before dawn, he left and went off to a deserted place, where he prayed. Simon and those who were with him pursued him and on finding him said, "Everyone is looking for you." He told them, "Let us go on to the nearby villages that I may preach there also. For this purpose have I come." So he went into their synagogues, preaching and driving out demons throughout the whole of Galilee.

Reflecting on the Word

Jesus' fame was spreading, and more and more people were seeking healing from him. Amid this frenzy, Jesus sought time in solitude with his Father. He arose early, went to a deserted place, and prayed. The time with God rejuvenated him, and once again he readied himself to preach to the people. Our lives are busy, but we need to seek out peace and quiet, so our hearts, minds, and spirits may be replenished and refocused to God's purpose in our lives.

•••••• ON THE WAY TO MASS

Is it quiet or loud when you pray?

ON THE WAY HOME FROM MASS ••••••

At Mass, was it quiet or loud when we prayed? How did you focus when you heard God speaking to us in the readings today?

Living the Word

Take time each day to listen to God's voice in prayer. Select a time that is suitable for all family members. Set up a prayer space in your home where family members may experience quiet prayer time. You might have small table on which you could place a Bible, candle, and a cross or prayer cards. Prepare your children to listen and to be comfortable in the silence by asking them a question to reflect on, such as "Where did you feel God's love today?" or "How might you follow Jesus more closely?" Start with a small amount of time and increase as you feel appropriate. Afterward, ask your children how they felt during prayer time.

February 14, 2021

Sixth Sunday in Ordinary Time

Hearing the Word

Mark 1:40–45

In the name of the Father, and of the Son, and of the Holy Spirit.

A leper came to Jesus and kneeling down begged him and said, "If you wish, you can make me clean." Moved with pity, he stretched out his hand, touched him, and said to him, "I do will it. Be made clean." The leprosy left him immediately, and he was made clean. Then, warning him sternly, he dismissed him at once.

Then he said to him, "See that you tell no one anything, but go, show yourself to the priest and offer for your cleansing what Moses prescribed; that will be proof for them."

The man went away and began to publicize the whole matter. He spread the report abroad so that it was impossible for Jesus to enter a town openly. He remained outside in deserted places, and people kept coming to him from everywhere.

Reflecting on the Word

Even though Jesus told the leper to tell no one, the leper cannot keep his healing a secret. Although the leper disobeyed Jesus, Jesus does not appear to be upset. Perhaps Jesus was aware of the man's humanity—it is easy to forgive sharing the good news out of pure joy and excitement! God's healing love is meant to be shared joyfully with all.

• • • • • • ON THE WAY TO MASS

Have you ever been so excited about something that you couldn't wait to tell everyone?

ON THE WAY HOME FROM MASS • • • • • •

If you were the leper, would you have listened to what Jesus said and not said anything, or would you have done as he did and told everyone you met? Why?

Living the Word

The leper trusted and had such faith that Jesus could heal him. With your children, try this experiment. Fill a resealable plastic bag with water. Holding it by the top, stick sharpened pencils all the way through the bag so that it pops through the other side. Add more pencils. Water should not leak from the bag. It takes a leap of faith to push a pencil through a bag of water and expect it not to spill everywhere. How can we trust Jesus as completely?

February 21, 2021

First Sunday of Lent

Hearing the Word
Mark 1:12–15

In the name of the Father, and of the Son, and of the Holy Spirit.

The Spirit drove Jesus out into the desert, and he remained in the desert for forty days, tempted by Satan. He was among wild beasts, and the angels ministered to him.

After John had been arrested, Jesus came to Galilee proclaiming the gospel of God: "This is the time of fulfillment. The kingdom of God is at hand. Repent, and believe in the gospel."

Reflecting on the Word

As we prepare for Easter, we are invited to a change of mind and heart during the season of Lent. We are asked to tend to our spiritual well-being by asking ourselves how we can be more kind, love more deeply, follow Jesus more closely, and begin a renewed, rejuvenated relationship with God. But we are also reminded by the three pillars of Lent—fasting, almsgiving, and prayer—to do more for others, to show solidarity with the poor, and to participate humbly in the works of charity.

•••••• ON THE WAY TO MASS

Explain to your children that we are now in the season of Lent. Ask them to notice the church environment. Prepare to explain that violet is the liturgical color of repentance and the worship environment is now simple and spare. The signs of festivity that are usually a part of the Sunday liturgy, such as the Gloria and Alleluia, are set aside during Lent.

ON THE WAY HOME FROM MASS ••••••

What did you notice about how the church looked today?

Living the Word

Observe the season of Lent by planning ways your family can give your time and talents to others. Ask your children for their input, and suggest other ideas that you could do as a family. Try to plan an activity for each week during Lent. How do these activities turn your hearts and minds toward God?

February 28, 2021

SECOND SUNDAY OF LENT

Hearing the Word
Mark 9:2–10

In the name of the Father, and of the Son, and of the Holy Spirit.

Jesus took Peter, James, and John and led them up a high mountain apart by themselves. And he was transfigured before them, and his clothes became dazzling white, such as no fuller on earth could bleach them. Then Elijah appeared to them along with Moses, and they were conversing with Jesus. Then Peter said to Jesus in reply, "Rabbi, it is good that we are here! Let us make three tents: one for you, one for Moses, and one for Elijah." He hardly knew what to say, they were so terrified. Then a cloud came, casting a shadow over them; from the cloud came a voice, "This is my beloved Son. Listen to him." Suddenly, looking around, they no longer saw anyone but Jesus alone with them.

As they were coming down from the mountain, he charged them not to relate what they had seen to anyone, except when the Son of Man had risen from the dead. So they kept the matter to themselves, questioning what rising from the dead meant.

Reflecting on the Word

Peter, James, and John received a glimpse into the glory and beauty of Christ during the Transfiguration. Peter experienced such a profound spiritual awakening that he wished to set up three tents for Moses, Elijah, and Jesus so that they could stay in that moment. But Jesus brought the disciples back down the mountain. We might experience a similar profound spiritual moment, whether in deep prayer, during Mass, or finding clarity during meditation. We might want to stay in that moment, but we must always return to our daily lives.

• • • • • • ON THE WAY TO MASS

Do you know what a transfiguration is?

ON THE WAY HOME FROM MASS • • • • • •

Explain that being transfigured means to change in appearance or shape. Jesus made his glory known to the disciples, but he wasn't changing who he was. Jesus was a man, but also fully divine.

Living the Word

Create a sun catcher using outlines of the figure of Jesus, card stock, wax paper, coloring materials, scissors, string, a hole punch, and tape. Trace the figure of Jesus on card stock and color the background. Cut the sun catcher in a circle shape and cut out the figure of Jesus. Next, tape a square of wax paper to the sun catcher and loop a length of string on it. Have your children hold up their sun catcher to the window or a lamp or flashlight. How do you think the disciples felt to see such a dazzling sight?

March 7, 2021

THIRD SUNDAY OF LENT

Hearing the Word
John 2:13–17

In the name of the Father, and of the Son, and of the Holy Spirit.

Since the Passover of the Jews was near, Jesus went up to Jerusalem. He found in the temple area those who sold oxen, sheep, and doves, as well as the money changers seated there. He made a whip out of cords and drove them all out of the temple area, with the sheep and oxen, and spilled the coins of the money changers and overturned their tables, and to those who sold doves he said, "Take these out of here, and stop making my Father's house a marketplace." His disciples recalled the words of Scripture, / *Zeal for your house will consume me.*

Reflecting on the Word

In this Gospel, Jesus reacts strongly to the business transactions in a place of God. He is angry, and that anger spills into physicality. When he perceived the temple, a place of prayer and worship to God, to be overrun with business dealings, he evaluates the situation to be degrading and diminishing to God and responds with anger. In that very human response, he validates our own human emotions. His anger led him to action—he removed the marketplace from the temple. We too, then, must take our strong emotions and respond appropriately. How can we take our anger, our love, our joy, and use them in a way that benefits God's Kingdom?

•••••• ON THE WAY TO MASS

Have you ever felt really angry? Is it a good feeling?

ON THE WAY HOME FROM MASS ••••••

How might we use our emotions in constructive ways?

Living the Word

Acting in anger can be destructive, so it's good to redirect it so that it fuels actions that are more constructive. Talk with your family about how to redirect feelings of anger. Does taking a deep breath help, or does it help to be alone for a while? Could you stick up for someone being bullied or left out? Could you take action on an issue for social justice? As a family, decide to take compassionate action this Lent.

March 14, 2021

Fourth Sunday of Lent

Hearing the Word
John 3:14–21

In the name of the Father, and of the Son, and of the Holy Spirit.

Jesus said to Nicodemus: "Just as Moses lifted up the serpent in the desert, so must the Son of Man be lifted up, so that everyone who believes in him may have eternal life."

For God so loved the world that he gave his only Son, so that everyone who believes in him might not perish but might have eternal life. For God did not send his Son into the world to condemn the world, but that the world might be saved through him. Whoever believes in him will not be condemned, but whoever does not believe has already been condemned, because he has not believed in the name of the only Son of God. And this is the verdict, that the light came into the world, but people preferred darkness to light, because their works were evil. For everyone who does wicked things hates the light and does not come toward the light, so that his works might not be exposed. But whoever lives the truth comes to the light, so that his works may be clearly seen as done in God.

Reflecting on the Word

Perhaps one of the most well-recited and reprinted verses in the New Testament is John 3:16: "For God so loved the world that he gave his only Son, so that everyone who believes in him might not perish but might have eternal life." God is the Creator who loved the world—not only Jesus, the disciples, and everyone who praised God, but all of creation. God's love is the simple and profound force that motivates the entire work of creation. God sent Jesus to us not to judge or condemn but to save. How do we respond to that awesome love?

•••••• ON THE WAY TO MASS

Why did Jesus become human?

ON THE WAY HOME FROM MASS ••••••

How can we bring Christ's light to others?

Living the Word

Prepare enough votive candles so that there is one for each family member. At your prayer space, light a candle for each person. As you do, invite other family members to talk about how God's love shines in that person and how he or she is a light to others. Continue as you light a candle for the next family member. Then praise and thank God for his love and goodness.

March 21, 2021

Fifth Sunday of Lent

Hearing the Word

John 12:20–33

In the name of the Father, and of the Son, and of the Holy Spirit.

Some Greeks who had come to worship at the Passover Feast came to Philip, who was from Bethsaida in Galilee, and asked him, "Sir, we would like to see Jesus." Philip went and told Andrew; then Andrew and Philip went and told Jesus. Jesus answered them, "The hour has come for the Son of Man to be glorified. Amen, amen, I say to you, unless a grain of wheat falls to the ground and dies, it remains just a grain of wheat; but if it dies, it produces much fruit. Whoever loves his life loses it, and whoever hates his life in this world will preserve it for eternal life. Whoever serves me must follow me, and where I am, there also will my servant be. The Father will honor whoever serves me.

"I am troubled now. Yet what should I say? 'Father, save me from this hour'? But it was for this purpose that I came to this hour. Father, glorify your name." Then a voice came from heaven, "I have glorified it and will glorify it again." The crowd there heard it and said it was thunder; but others said, "An angel has spoken to him." Jesus answered and said, "This voice did not come for my sake but for yours. Now is the time of judgment on this world; now the ruler of this world will be driven out. And when I am lifted up from the earth, I will draw everyone to myself." He said this indicating the kind of death he would die.

Reflecting on the Word

In the parable of the grain of wheat, Jesus predicts his own death and Resurrection. The life of the wheat begins with the death of its seed. New wheat soon flourishes, and with the appropriate care and attention, it will bear much fruit. Jesus will die on the cross but will soon rise again to a new life, and through him we will share in that eternal life. We too must remove whatever prevents us from flourishing in God's love and living a Christ-centered life.

•••••• ON THE WAY TO MASS

How do seeds grow? What is necessary for the plant to thrive?

ON THE WAY HOME FROM MASS ••••••

How can we nourish our hearts and minds to grow?

Living the Word

Observe the lifecycle of seeds with your children by growing some grass at home. Fill small pots (or paper cups) with planting soil, and add grass seeds. Place your pots in an area where sun shines. Give your children the responsibility of watering the plants on a regular basis. Observe the plants daily and discuss how they are growing. (You might want your children to keep a daily record of their observations.) What do the plants need to grow? What do we need to grow in faith?

March 28, 2021

Palm Sunday of the Passion of the Lord

Hearing the Word

Mark 11:1–2, 7–10

In the name of the Father, and of the Son, and of the Holy Spirit.

When Jesus and his disciples drew near to Jerusalem, to Bethpage and Bethany at the Mount of Olives, he sent two of his disciples and said to them, "Go into the village opposite you, and immediately on entering it, you will find a colt tethered on which no one has ever sat. Untie it and bring it here." So they brought the colt to Jesus and put their cloaks over it. And he sat on it. Many of the people spread their cloaks on the road, and others spread leafy branches that they had cut from the fields. Those preceding him as well as those following kept crying out: / "Hosanna! / Blessed is he who comes in the name of the Lord! / Blessed is the kingdom of our father David that is to come! / Hosanna in the highest!"

Reflecting on the Word

On Palm Sunday, we are reminded of how Jesus triumphantly returned to Jerusalem. In today's liturgy, we also process into church, holding palms and singing. This is a celebratory reception filled with praise, adoration, and great joy. Jesus' welcome into the city was in stark contrast to what will take place on Good Friday.

•••••• ON THE WAY TO MASS

How would we welcome Jesus into our town or church if he were to arrive today?

ON THE WAY HOME FROM MASS ••••••

Plan to attend any or all of the Holy Week liturgies: Holy Thursday, Good Friday, and the Easter Vigil.

Living the Word

Today begins the holiest week of the liturgical year. As a reminder of what this week is about, place your blessed palms in your prayer space. Leave small slips of paper on your prayer table and invite family members to write something they hope for on one side of the slip, and then something they fear on the other side. Encourage them to write on the slips for the entire week. On Saturday night, when the Easter fire is lighted, burn these papers to symbolize that your family is giving these hopes and fears over to God.

April 4, 2021

Easter Sunday of the Resurrection of the Lord

Hearing the Word

Mark 16:1-7

In the name of the Father, and of the Son, and of the Holy Spirit.

When the sabbath was over, Mary Magdalene, Mary, the mother of James, and Salome bought spices so that they might go and anoint him. Very early when the sun had risen, on the first day of the week, they came to the tomb. They were saying to one another, "Who will roll back the stone for us from the entrance to the tomb?" When they looked up, they saw that the stone had been rolled back; it was very large. On entering the tomb they saw a young man sitting on the right side, clothed in a white robe, and they were utterly amazed. He said to them, "Do not be amazed! You seek Jesus of Nazareth, the crucified. He has been raised; he is not here. Behold the place where they laid him. But go and tell his disciples and Peter, 'He is going before you to Galilee; there you will see him, as he told you.'"

Reflecting on the Word

Alleluia! Jesus Christ is risen! Mary Magdalene, Mary the mother of James, and Salome were utterly amazed at witnessing the empty tomb and being told that Jesus had been raised. Although we know Jesus has conquered death, and we celebrate his Resurrection at Mass every week, today especially we celebrate that death has no power over Jesus! Alleluia!

••••••ON THE WAY TO MASS

We are celebrating Easter Sunday today. Why is today the most special day of the church year?

ON THE WAY HOME FROM MASS ••••••

How did you feel during Mass today? Name some emotions.

Living the Word

Sometime this week, have your children draw and color their memory of your church community on Easter Sunday. Recall with them the smiles on the faces of the assembly, the fancy Easter attire, the lilies and the colors of the worship space, the smells of incense, the feel of the holy water. What other memories do they have of the Easter celebration? Display the art in a place where your children can view it frequently to remember the great celebration and joy of Easter.

April 11, 2021

SECOND SUNDAY OF EASTER / SUNDAY OF DIVINE MERCY

Hearing the Word

John 20:19–23

In the name of the Father, and of the Son, and of the Holy Spirit.

On the evening of that first day of the week, when the doors were locked, where the disciples were, for fear of the Jews, Jesus came and stood in their midst and said to them, "Peace be with you." When he had said this, he showed them his hands and his side. The disciples rejoiced when they saw the Lord. Jesus said to them again, "Peace be with you. As the Father has sent me, so I send you." And when he had said this, he breathed on them and said to them, "Receive the Holy Spirit. Whose sins you forgive are forgiven them, and whose sins you retain are retained."

Reflecting on the Word

Jesus reveals himself to the disciples and immediately offers them peace—not once, but twice. How comforting that must have been after hiding in fear. Peace and forgiveness were so integral to the work of Jesus. Is it ever possible to attain peace in our heart, soul, and mind without both asking for forgiveness and forgiving others? What a crushing burden it would be in our hearts if we could not trust in a merciful God.

• • • • • • ON THE WAY TO MASS

Why do we give the Sign of Peace at Mass? What does this gesture mean?

ON THE WAY HOME FROM MASS • • • • • •

Can you say "Peace be with you" to individuals outside Mass? Why or why not? How would that make you feel? How would it make them feel?

Living the Word

Jesus sent his disciples to forgive sins. Practice forgiving others and asking for forgiveness by making it a central part of your family's prayer life this week. Begin by talking with your family about how important it is to forgive others, and how necessary it is to ask for forgiveness when we've done something wrong or hurt someone. Remind them gently each morning, and talk about it again before bed. Did they have to ask anyone for forgiveness today? Or did they forget? Did they forgive others when they've been hurt? How did it make them feel?

April 18, 2021

Third Sunday of Easter

Hearing the Word

Luke 24:36–40, 44–48

In the name of the Father, and of the Son, and of the Holy Spirit.

[Jesus] stood in their midst and said to them, "Peace be with you." But they were startled and terrified and thought that they were seeing a ghost. Then he said to them, "Why are you troubled? And why do questions arise in your hearts? Look at my hands and my feet, that it is I myself. Touch me and see, because a ghost does not have flesh and bones as you can see I have." And as he said this, he showed them his hands and his feet.

He said to them, "These are my words that I spoke to you while I was still with you, that everything written about me in the law of Moses and in the prophets and psalms must be fulfilled." Then he opened their minds to understand the Scriptures. And he said to them, "Thus it is written that the Christ would suffer and rise from the dead on the third day and that repentance, for the forgiveness of sins, would be preached in his name to all the nations, beginning from Jerusalem. You are witnesses of these things."

Reflecting on the Word

Once again we hear, this time from Luke, that Jesus' first words to his disciples after his Resurrection were "Peace be with you." How important that phrase is! When we share the Sign of Peace during Mass, we are remembering that true peace can only come from one source. When our souls are at peace, we are unafraid and able to listen and follow the voice of God.

......ON THE WAY TO MASS

What does it mean to feel "at peace"? Have you ever felt that way?

ON THE WAY HOME FROM MASS ......

Can we continue to wish people peace outside of Mass? If you didn't try it last week, can you try this week?

Living the Word

Peace is a theme in much of the music we sing at Mass and in many catechesis programs as well. Ask your children if they know any songs that have the word *peace* in them, or find songs from Mass (for example, "Prayer for Peace," "Peace Is Flowing like a River," "Let There Be Peace on Earth," "Make Me a Channel of Your Peace," and so on). If your children are old enough to read, choose a song and copy the lyrics on a poster board. Practice singing the songs daily. Include them in your prayers before bed or as the children are getting ready for their day. Let these songs fill your hearts and help your family bring the peace of God into your lives.

April 25, 2021

Fourth Sunday of Easter

Hearing the Word

John 10:11–18

In the name of the Father, and of the Son, and of the Holy Spirit.

Jesus said: "I am the good shepherd. A good shepherd lays down his life for the sheep. A hired man, who is not a shepherd and whose sheep are not his own, sees a wolf coming and leaves the sheep and runs away, and the wolf catches and scatters them. This is because he works for pay and has no concern for the sheep. I am the good shepherd, and I know mine and mine know me, just as the Father knows me and I know the Father; and I will lay down my life for the sheep. I have other sheep that do not belong to this fold. These also I must lead, and they will hear my voice, and there will be one flock, one shepherd. This is why the Father loves me, because I lay down my life in order to take it up again. No one takes it from me, but I lay it down on my own. I have power to lay it down, and power to take it up again. This command I have received from my Father."

Reflecting on the Word

The image of the Good Shepherd as a portrait of God's love for us is one of the most beloved in Scripture. Jesus knows all his sheep, cares for them, and will lay down his life for any of them. How amazing it is to know that Jesus loves and cares for us so much, and that we are all treasured, not for what we possess or what we create, but simply for being one of his flock.

······ ON THE WAY TO MASS

What does a shepherd do? Why is Jesus called the Good Shepherd?

ON THE WAY HOME FROM MASS ······

What does Jesus mean when he says we will all be of one flock?

Living the Word

Go online and find an image of Jesus the Good Shepherd. Display it where your children may focus on it for a moment. Ask them to look at the picture and tell you what they see. Then read aloud Psalm 23, verses 1–4, from your Bible. Ask your family to reflect on the following questions: What feelings do the images of the Good Shepherd conjure? How would you feel if you were one of his sheep?

May 2, 2021

Fifth Sunday of Easter

Hearing the Word

John 15:1–8

In the name of the Father, and of the Son, and of the Holy Spirit.

Jesus said to his disciples: "I am the true vine, and my Father is the vine grower. He takes away every branch in me that does not bear fruit, and every one that does he prunes so that it bears more fruit. You are already pruned because of the word that I spoke to you. Remain in me, as I remain in you. Just as a branch cannot bear fruit on its own unless it remains on the vine, so neither can you unless you remain in me. I am the vine, you are the branches. Whoever remains in me and I in him will bear much fruit, because without me you can do nothing. Anyone who does not remain in me will be thrown out like a branch and wither; people will gather them and throw them into a fire and they will be burned. If you remain in me and my words remain in you, ask for whatever you want and it will be done for you. By this is my Father glorified, that you bear much fruit and become my disciples."

Reflecting on the Word

Jesus is the one true vine, flowing through us—creating, connecting, and nourishing us. When we are broken or cut off from Jesus, we wither. If we remain connected to Jesus, the source from which all goodness flows, we keep him as the center of our lives always. We must choose to be connected to God every day.

•••••• ON THE WAY TO MASS

What does it mean to "remain" in someone? Listen for that word in today's Gospel. How many times is it spoken?

ON THE WAY HOME FROM MASS ••••••

How many times did you hear the word *remain* in the Gospel? Explain what it means.

Living the Word

If you have a houseplant, place it on a table. Have the children observe the plant. Which part is the "vine"? Which are the "branches"? What is the "fruit"? How are they connected? What makes them grow? Which part of the plant is Jesus? Which part are we? Which part comes out of us because of our connection with Jesus (for example, what we do, say, or think). With cotton swabs or cotton balls and a small bowl of water, have the children gently wipe the leaves clean. How can we take care of ourselves and be ready for Jesus? What would happen if we split the plant to grow in two pots? Would the second plant still be part of the same vine?

May 9, 2021

Sixth Sunday of Easter

Hearing the Word

John 15:9–17

In the name of the Father, and of the Son, and of the Holy Spirit.

Jesus said to his disciples: "As the Father loves me, so I also love you. Remain in my love. If you keep my commandments, you will remain in my love, just as I have kept my Father's commandments and remain in his love.

"I have told you this so that my joy may be in you and your joy might be complete. This is my commandment: love one another as I love you. No one has greater love than this, to lay down one's life for one's friends. You are my friends if you do what I command you. I no longer call you slaves, because a slave does not know what his master is doing. I have called you friends, because I have told you everything I have heard from my Father. It was not you who chose me, but I who chose you and appointed you to go and bear fruit that will remain, so that whatever you ask the Father in my name he may give you. This I command you: love one another."

Reflecting on the Word

It is still Easter Time. Are we still celebrating? In today's Gospel, we are reminded about love. Jesus loves us and asks us to remain in his love, just as he remains in his Father's love. Jesus finds great joy in loving us, and his love should bring us great joy! Jesus asks us to love not only him, but to love one another. Repeatedly, the Gospel narratives remind us that love is the central mission of Jesus. As he says here, we did not choose him, but he chose us! That is something to celebrate!

• • • • • • ON THE WAY TO MASS

What are God's commandments? Which ones do you remember and keep?

ON THE WAY HOME FROM MASS • • • • • •

Do you think Jesus' commandment to love is different from or the same as the Ten Commandments? Why?

Living the Word

Jesus asks us to love one another. How can we show people close to us that we love them? How can we show someone that we don't know very well that we love him or her too? Gather some ideas with your children and put them into action. We human beings experience love primarily through the power of appropriate touch. Share a hug or snuggle, or show support to someone with a hand on the shoulder or a simple handshake. Let us find great joy in loving others!

May 13/16, 2021

Solemnity of the Ascension of the Lord

Hearing the Word

Mark 16:15–20

In the name of the Father, and of the Son, and of the Holy Spirit.

Jesus said to his disciples: "Go into the whole world and proclaim the gospel to every creature. Whoever believes and is baptized will be saved; whoever does not believe will be condemned. These signs will accompany those who believe: in my name they will drive out demons, they will speak new languages. They will pick up serpents with their hands, and if they drink any deadly thing, it will not harm them. They will lay hands on the sick, and they will recover."

So then the Lord Jesus, after he spoke to them, was taken up into heaven and took his seat at the right hand of God. But they went forth and preached everywhere, while the Lord worked with them and confirmed the word through accompanying signs.

Reflecting on the Word

Today we celebrate Christ going back to his Father in heaven. Before being taken up, Jesus instructed his disciples to proclaim the Gospel to every creature. He said there would be "signs" accompanying those who believed, and even after ascending into heaven, the Lord continued to work with his disciples and confirmed what they were doing with signs. What signs do we experience that tell us we are on the right path? Are they visible signs or feelings? How can we take the time to recognize these signs that God is present throughout the day?

•••••• ON THE WAY TO MASS

What does the word *ascension* mean?

ON THE WAY HOME FROM MASS ••••••

Jesus gave his disciples (among whom we are included) some instruction before he ascended to heaven. What does Jesus mean by preaching the Gospel to every creature?

Living the Word

Find a simple reading from the Bible (last week's Gospel on loving one another as Jesus has loved us is a great one!). Help your children read the passage (or a shorter version of it) to their pets, plants, in your backyard, or at a park. Do this several days in a row. How do the children find reading to animals, plants, or in nature when they do not get a response? Why did Jesus want his followers to proclaim the Gospel to all of creation? How can we take care of God's creation?

May 16, 2021

Seventh Sunday of Easter

Hearing the Word

John 17:11b–19

In the name of the Father, and of the Son, and of the Holy Spirit.

Lifting up his eyes to heaven, Jesus prayed saying: "Holy
Father, keep them in your name that you have given me,
so that they may be one just as we are one. When I was with
them I protected them in your name that you gave me, and
I guarded them, and none of them was lost except the son
of destruction, in order that the Scripture might be fulfilled.
But now I am coming to you. I speak this in the world so
that they may share my joy completely. I gave them your word,
and the world hated them, because they do not belong to the
world any more than I belong to the world. I do not ask that
you take them out of the world but that you keep them from
the evil one. They do not belong to the world any more than
I belong to the world. Consecrate them in the truth. Your
word is truth. As you sent me into the world, so I sent them
into the world. And I consecrate myself for them, so that they
also may be consecrated in truth."

Reflecting on the Word

As we near the end of Easter Time, Jesus prays to God for his disciples. He prays that they are united as one, that they share completely in Jesus' joy, that they are protected from evil, and that they are washed in God's truth. Jesus clearly loved his disciples and interceded with the Father on their behalf, so that they would continue to be protected and united even after he ascended into heaven. Jesus acknowledges that the world is not on their side, but he is. How Jesus cares for his relationship with his followers! How can we respond to that loving care?

...... ON THE WAY TO MASS

How do you think Jesus must have felt to leave his disciples behind on earth?

ON THE WAY HOME FROM MASS ......

Do you think Jesus prays for you? How does that make you feel?

Living the Word

Jesus gave us the words to pray to God in the Our Father. How can we pray together as one, as Jesus wanted? This week, pray the Our Father together. Hold hands in a circle as you pray. What else would unite Jesus' followers?

May 23, 2021

Pentecost Sunday

Hearing the Word

John 15:26–27; 16:12–15

In the name of the Father, and of the Son, and of the Holy Spirit.

Jesus said to his disciples: "When the Advocate comes whom I will send you from the Father, the Spirit of truth that proceeds from the Father, he will testify to me. And you also testify, because you have been with me from the beginning.

"I have much more to tell you, but you cannot bear it now. But when he comes, the Spirit of truth, he will guide you to all truth. He will not speak on his own, but he will speak what he hears, and will declare to you the things that are coming. He will glorify me, because he will take from what is mine and declare it to you. Everything that the Father has is mine; for this reason I told you that he will take from what is mine and declare it to you."

Reflecting on the Word

Today we celebrate Pentecost Sunday, the coming of the Holy Spirit (or "Advocate") to the disciples. The Holy Spirit will guide us to truth and will help us live as Jesus called us to live. The Spirit is all around us and speaks truth to us every day. How can we acknowledge and respond to the presence of the Holy Spirit in our lives?

•••••• ON THE WAY TO MASS

Who is the Holy Spirit?

ON THE WAY HOME FROM MASS ••••••

Do you ever feel the presence of the Holy Spirit or hear the Spirit talk to you?

Living the Word

The Holy Spirit can be a difficult concept for young children to understand since we cannot see the Holy Spirit. Wind is often used to describe the Holy Spirit because it can be as soft as a whisper and as strong as a hurricane. We know that the wind can be powerful and move things, and it can be a gentle presence in our lives as well. A pinwheel is a helpful way for the children to understand the power of the wind. When a child blows on a pinwheel, it turns even faster. Have the children decorate their pinwheels with red (a color associated with the Holy Spirit) markers and assemble them. Place the pinwheels outside in the ground or in an open window to remind them of the Holy Spirit this Pentecost Sunday.

May 30, 2021

Solemnity of the Most Holy Trinity

Hearing the Word

Matthew 28:16–20

In the name of the Father, and of the Son, and of the Holy Spirit.

The eleven disciples went to Galilee, to the mountain to which Jesus had ordered them. When they all saw him, they worshiped, but they doubted. Then Jesus approached and said to them, "All power in heaven and on earth has been given to me. Go, therefore, and make disciples of all nations, baptizing them in the name of the Father, and of the Son, and of the Holy Spirit, teaching them to observe all that I have commanded you. And behold, I am with you always, until the end of the age."

Reflecting on the Word

In today's Gospel, we hear from Jesus how to baptize in the Persons of the Trinity. We invoke the Trinity not only when we baptize, but also when we make the Sign of the Cross. Praying in the name of the Father, and of the Son, and of the Holy Spirit enables us to center ourselves, our thoughts, and our prayers toward God. It also reminds us that God is present in all our daily lives.

•••••• ON THE WAY TO MASS

When you pray, do you think of God the Father, Jesus, or the Holy Spirit?

ON THE WAY HOME FROM MASS ••••••

When do we most often say, "In the name of the Father, Son, and Holy Spirit"? What does it mean to begin and end our prayers in this way?

Living the Word

Throughout the centuries, there have been many names for the three Persons of the Holy Trinity. For example, God is called Father, Mother, Creator; the Son is called Redeemer and Beloved; and the Holy Spirit is called Sustainer and Love. Create with your children a chart with three sections and list new names that help your children identify with the Persons of the Trinity. Look to the Bible and Catholic artwork to help with this. Which name do you identify with most?

June 6, 2021

Solemnity of the Most Holy Body and Blood of Christ

Hearing the Word

Mark 14:12–16, 22–26

In the name of the Father, and of the Son, and of the Holy Spirit.

On the first day of the Feast of Unleavened Bread, when they sacrificed the Passover lamb, Jesus' disciples said to him, "Where do you want us to go and prepare for you to eat the Passover?" He sent two of his disciples and said to them, "Go into the city and a man will meet you, carrying a jar of water. Follow him. Wherever he enters, say to the master of the house, 'The Teacher says, "Where is my guest room where I may eat the Passover with my disciples?"' Then he will show you a large upper room furnished and ready. Make the preparations for us there." The disciples then went off, entered the city, and found it just as he had told them; and they prepared the Passover.

While they were eating, he took bread, said the blessing, broke it, gave it to them, and said, "Take it; this is my body." Then he took a cup, gave thanks, and gave it to them, and they all drank from it. He said to them, "This is my blood of the covenant, which will be shed for many. Amen, I say to you, I shall not drink again the fruit of the vine until the day when I drink it new in the kingdom of God." Then, after singing a hymn, they went out to the Mount of Olives.

Reflecting on the Word

In today's Gospel, the disciples are asked to prepare for the Passover meal, and they actively do so. When we receive the Body and Blood of Christ at Communion, we imitate that Passover meal Jesus shared with his disciples. We welcome Christ not only into our presence, but also into our bodies in a very intimate way. But just like the disciples, we need to prepare ourselves and our surroundings for Christ's presence. We need to prepare our bodies and our souls for Christ's presence. How full of wonder and thanksgiving we should be to welcome him into our lives in such a way!

•••••• ON THE WAY TO MASS

Ask your children to notice how the lay ministers prepare the table.

ON THE WAY HOME FROM MASS ••••••

Ask your family to share their observations during the Liturgy of the Eucharist. In what ways can your family help at Mass in the future?

Living the Word

On today's solemnity, prepare your own table as though Jesus were coming to break bread with you. Ask your children to help you lay a fancy tablecloth and tableware and set flowers or candles to create an atmosphere of hospitality and formality to your meal. As you dine together, ask how you would serve Jesus. What conversations would you have if Jesus were present?

June 13, 2021

Eleventh Sunday in Ordinary Time

Hearing the Word

Mark 4:26–34

In the name of the Father, and of the Son, and of the Holy Spirit.

Jesus said to the crowds: "This is how it is with the kingdom of God; it is as if a man were to scatter seed on the land and would sleep and rise night and day and through it all the seed would sprout and grow, he knows not how. Of its own accord the land yields fruit, first the blade, then the ear, then the full grain in the ear. And when the grain is ripe, he wields the sickle at once, for the harvest has come."

He said, "To what shall we compare the kingdom of God, or what parable can we use for it? It is like a mustard seed that, when it is sown in the ground, is the smallest of all the seeds on the earth. But once it is sown, it springs up and becomes the largest of plants and puts forth large branches, so that the birds of the sky can dwell in its shade." With many such parables he spoke the word to them as they were able to understand it. Without parables he did not speak to them, but to his own disciples he explained everything in private.

Reflecting on the Word

We are back in Ordinary Time and learn more from Jesus. Today, he compares the Kingdom of God to a mustard seed. Jesus tells us that even something as small as a mustard seed can grow into something enormous. Each seed, each person in the Kingdom of God, is valuable and significant.

• • • • • • ON THE WAY TO MASS

Can just one person, even those as young as you, make a difference? How?

ON THE WAY HOME FROM MASS • • • • • •

What does the growth of the mustard seed tell us about what we, and the Church, need to do to help grow the Kingdom of God?

Living the Word

Find a mustard seed to show your children what Jesus was referring to in today's Gospel. (Or go online to find a picture.) Ask your family why Jesus would have used this seed as an example to teach about the potential each of us has in God's Kingdom. What small things can each of us do that will have a big impact on someone else?

June 20, 2021

Twelfth Sunday in Ordinary Time

Hearing the Word
Mark 4:35–41

In the name of the Father, and of the Son, and of the Holy Spirit.

On that day, as evening drew on, Jesus said to his disciples: "Let us cross to the other side." Leaving the crowd, they took Jesus with them in the boat just as he was. And other boats were with him. A violent squall came up and waves were breaking over the boat, so that it was already filling up. Jesus was in the stern, asleep on a cushion. They woke him and said to him, "Teacher, do you not care that we are perishing?" He woke up, rebuked the wind, and said to the sea, "Quiet! Be still!" The wind ceased and there was great calm. Then he asked them, "Why are you terrified? Do you not yet have faith?" They were filled with great awe and said to one another, "Who then is this whom even wind and sea obey?"

Reflecting on the Word

The disciples were terrified they were going to die during a storm at sea. It is human to be frightened like the disciples were, to feel alone because God was sleeping. It is also part of being human to experience some rough seas—our lives have moments of disaster and storms. But we are reminded in this Gospel that God is always present. God is there, waiting to be called on for help and comfort. We need to remember in our most difficult moments to ask God to be with us so that we never feel alone.

......ON THE WAY TO MASS

Have you ever experienced a rough, awful day or moment where you really felt alone? Did you ever ask anyone for help?

ON THE WAY HOME FROM MASS ......

We hear that Jesus was able to calm the sea and wind. Do you call on Jesus to calm you when you are afraid?

Living the Word

Jesus is always with us, but we need to be reminded of his presence often. This week, ask your children whether they felt Jesus' presence, especially when they experienced challenging or bad days. Did they remember that Jesus was always near and waiting to be called upon? Did they pray? Think of ways to remind them of Jesus' presence.

June 27, 2021

THIRTEENTH SUNDAY IN ORDINARY TIME

Hearing the Word

Mark 5:22–24, 35b–43

In the name of the Father, and of the Son, and of the Holy Spirit.

One of the synagogue officials, named Jairus, came forward. Seeing him he fell at his feet and pleaded earnestly with him, saying, "My daughter is at the point of death. Please, come lay your hands on her that she may get well and live." He went off with him, and a large crowd followed him and pressed upon him.

While he was still speaking, people from the synagogue official's house arrived and said, "Your daughter has died; why trouble the teacher any longer?" Disregarding the message that was reported, Jesus said to the synagogue official, "Do not be afraid; just have faith." He did not allow anyone to accompany him inside except Peter, James, and John, the brother of James. When they arrived at the house of the synagogue official, he caught sight of a commotion, people weeping and wailing loudly. So he went in and said to them, "Why this commotion and weeping? The child is not dead but asleep." And they ridiculed him. Then he put them all out. He took along the child's father and mother and those who were with him and entered the room where the child was. He took the child by the hand and said to her, *"Talitha koum,"* which means, "Little girl, I say to you, arise!" The girl, a child of twelve, arose immediately and walked around. At that they were utterly astounded. He gave strict orders that no one should know this and said that she should be given something to eat.

Reflecting on the Word

Jairus begs Jesus to heal his daughter. Even after receiving word that she has died, Jesus tells the members of the synagogue official's house, "Do not be afraid; just have faith." How can we, in our darkest times, with people telling us it's not possible, *just have faith*?

......ON THE WAY TO MASS

How would you describe your faith?

ON THE WAY HOME FROM MASS ......

How can we remember to ask Jesus for help when we are afraid?

Living the Word

Let the phrase "Just have faith" be your family's motto for the week. Whenever anyone is struggling or feeling afraid, sad, or disappointed, remind them to "Just have faith." You and your children might create a sign to be displayed in a common area in your home. Say it often to one another so that it becomes ingrained in your children's minds and hearts.

July 4, 2021

Fourteenth Sunday in Ordinary Time

Hearing the Word

Mark 6:1–6

In the name of the Father, and of the Son, and of the Holy Spirit.

Jesus departed from there and came to his native place, accompanied by his disciples. When the sabbath came he began to teach in the synagogue, and many who heard him were astonished. They said, "Where did this man get all this? What kind of wisdom has been given him? What mighty deeds are wrought by his hands! Is he not the carpenter, the son of Mary, and the brother of James and Joses and Judas and Simon? And are not his sisters here with us?" And they took offense at him. Jesus said to them, "A prophet is not without honor except in his native place and among his own kin and in his own house." So he was not able to perform any mighty deed there, apart from curing a few sick people by laying his hands on them. He was amazed at their lack of faith.

Reflecting on the Word

At the beginning of his ministry, Jesus arrived in Nazareth, and those who knew him as a child and watched him grow up were astonished by his teachings. But their astonishment quickly turned into anger, perhaps jealousy, and rejection. They "took offense at him." How sad Jesus must have felt to be rejected by those who knew him best! Despite this personal rejection, Jesus didn't need their approval and continued with his ministry.

......ON THE WAY TO MASS

Have you ever been rejected before? How did it make you feel?

ON THE WAY HOME FROM MASS ......

How can you support your friends and loved ones and their talents?

Living the Word

Hold a talent show in your home! Have each family member prepare a small demonstration (singing, dancing, reading, telling jokes, and so on). Select a night for the big "show," and prepare a stage or backdrop for the show. Have someone emcee the production and introduce each person for the family. Celebrate afterward with a special dessert, and talk about how it felt to perform in front of a supportive audience. Then recall the Sunday Gospel: How do you think Jesus felt when no one from his hometown appreciated his talents? How do you think that make him feel? How would you feel if did not get any cheers and applause?

July 11, 2021

Fifteenth Sunday in Ordinary Time

Hearing the Word

Mark 6:7–13

In the name of the Father, and of the Son, and of the Holy Spirit.

Jesus summoned the Twelve and began to send them out two by two and gave them authority over unclean spirits. He instructed them to take nothing for the journey but a walking stick—no food, no sack, no money in their belts. They were, however, to wear sandals but not a second tunic. He said to them, "Wherever you enter a house, stay there until you leave. Whatever place does not welcome you or listen to you, leave there and shake the dust off your feet in testimony against them." So they went off and preached repentance. The Twelve drove out many demons, and they anointed with oil many who were sick and cured them.

Reflecting on the Word

The disciples were sent, unburdened with baggage or belongings, and with very little in the way of power and prestige. They were given authority only in driving out unclean spirits and healing the sick. This humility allows them to serve God rather than serving themselves or their own agenda. They were sent two by two. They were not meant to travel and serve alone—they were meant to have companionship and support along their way.

••••••ON THE WAY TO MASS

Do you ever feel weighed down? Reflect silently on what burdens are in your heart and bring them to God.

ON THE WAY HOME FROM MASS ••••••

Jesus knew the assignment would not be easy, so he sent his disciples out in pairs. What does that tell you about Jesus' care and understanding?

Living the Word

Followers of Jesus were—and are—meant to stand together, to encourage and help one another, and to share the good news with each other. Call a local assisted-living facility, and ask how your family might help the patients. Could you share your time or companionship? Find a time where your family can go and visit, and care for the patients in some way. Perhaps you cannot heal physical wounds, but you can heal their spirits!

July 18, 2021

Sixteenth Sunday in Ordinary Time

Hearing the Word

Mark 6:30–34

In the name of the Father, and of the Son, and of the Holy Spirit.

The apostles gathered together with Jesus and reported all they had done and taught. He said to them, "Come away by yourselves to a deserted place and rest a while." People were coming and going in great numbers, and they had no opportunity even to eat. So they went off in the boat by themselves to a deserted place. People saw them leaving and many came to know about it. They hastened there on foot from all the towns and arrived at the place before them.

When he disembarked and saw the vast crowd, his heart was moved with pity for them, for they were like sheep without a shepherd; and he began to teach them many things.

Reflecting on the Word

Once again, we see Jesus as a good shepherd who cares for his flock. First, Jesus notices his disciples are worn out and invites his inner flock to "come away" and "rest awhile." He is compassionate, caring, and understanding of the demands of discipleship. But the people still needed Jesus, and they had sought him on foot. Moved with pity, Jesus is once again a shepherd, caring and teaching his larger flock.

• • • • • • ON THE WAY TO MASS

Do you sometimes feel like you need to sleep in and not go to Mass on Sundays?

ON THE WAY HOME FROM MASS • • • • • •

How do you feel after going to church? Are you still tired? Do you still need rest? Do you feel at all rejuvenated?

Living the Word

Choose a one- or two-hour period during the week (or even a full day if possible) and turn off all electronics. Avoid going online, playing computer games, watching television, or checking your smartphones. Use the time to refocus, rest, and perhaps meditate on Scripture together. How did this time make each of you feel? Could it be something you can fit into your weekly schedule?

July 25, 2021

Seventeenth Sunday in Ordinary Time

Hearing the Word

John 6:5–14

In the name of the Father, and of the Son, and of the Holy Spirit.

When Jesus raised his eyes and saw that a large crowd was coming to him, he said to Philip, "Where can we buy enough food for them to eat?" He said this to test him, because he himself knew what he was going to do. Philip answered him, "Two hundred days' wages worth of food would not be enough for each of them to have a little." One of his disciples, Andrew, the brother of Simon Peter, said to him, "There is a boy here who has five barley loaves and two fish; but what good are these for so many?" Jesus said, "Have the people recline." Now there was a great deal of grass in that place. So the men reclined, about five thousand in number. Then Jesus took the loaves, gave thanks, and distributed them to those who were reclining, and also as much of the fish as they wanted. When they had had their fill, he said to his disciples, "Gather the fragments left over, so that nothing will be wasted." So they collected them, and filled twelve wicker baskets with fragments from the five barley loaves that had been more than they could eat. When the people saw the sign he had done, they said, "This is truly the Prophet, the one who is to come into the world."

Reflecting on the Word

The multiplication of the loaves and fishes is the only miracle recorded in all four Gospel narratives. Today, it's hard sometimes to find miracles in everyday life because we often rationalize them or use science to explain them. But the miracle of the loaves and fishes must have been a story retold many times for all the evangelists to have a similar account of it. Often when we read the Gospel narratives, we learn that Jesus' followers were astonished or amazed. Can we too read this Gospel as the Good News, as a genuine miracle, and be astonished and amazed at how Jesus took five loaves of bread and two fish and fed five thousand?

······ ON THE WAY TO MASS

What is a miracle? Have you experienced or heard of one recently?

ON THE WAY HOME FROM MASS ······

If you were one of the 5,000 who had been fed by Jesus, how would you have felt?

Living the Word

Help your children understand the amount of 5,000. Gather various items from around the house in quantities of 100 each, for example, 100 cotton balls, 100 buttons, 100 pieces of cereal, or 100 stickers. Try to gather 10 sets of those items to total 1,000. Lay everything out on a large table. Can you imagine Jesus feeding five times that many people with just five loaves and two fishes? What a miracle that must have been to witness!

August 1, 2021

Eighteenth Sunday in Ordinary Time

Hearing the Word

John 6:26–35

In the name of the Father, and of the Son, and of the Holy Spirit.

[Jesus said,] "Amen, amen, I say to you, you are looking for me not because you saw signs but because you ate the loaves and were filled. Do not work for food that perishes but for the food that endures for eternal life, which the Son of Man will give you. For on him the Father, God, has set his seal." So they said to him, "What can we do to accomplish the works of God?" Jesus answered and said to them, "This is the work of God, that you believe in the one he sent." So they said to him, "What sign can you do, that we may see and believe in you? What can you do? Our ancestors ate manna in the desert, as it is written: *He gave them bread from heaven to eat.*" So Jesus said to them, "Amen, amen, I say to you, it was not Moses who gave the bread from heaven; my Father gives you the true bread from heaven. For the bread of God is that which comes down from heaven and gives life to the world."

So they said to him, "Sir, give us this bread always." Jesus said to them, "I am the bread of life; whoever comes to me will never hunger, and whoever believes in me will never thirst."

Reflecting on the Word

In this week's Gospel, we continue with more talk of bread. Jesus tells us that we need more than physical nourishment. We need sustenance for our soul. God gives life to us and gives us the essentials to live, not just for our time on earth, but for eternal life. Jesus gives us a profound statement: "I am the bread of life; whoever comes to me will never hunger, and whoever believes in me will never thirst."

•••••• ON THE WAY TO MASS

Have you ever heard the saying "You are what you eat"? What does that mean?

ON THE WAY HOME FROM MASS ••••••

How does Jesus Christ nourish us?

Living the Word

Talk about what you think the "true bread from heaven" is like. How does Jesus nourish you? What ingredients do we need to do the works of God? How is Jesus the bread of life? How does bread from heaven give life to the world?

August 8, 2021

Nineteenth Sunday in Ordinary Time

Hearing the Word

John 6:41–51

In the name of the Father, and of the Son, and of the Holy Spirit.

The Jews murmured about Jesus because he said, "I am the bread that came down from heaven," and they said, "Is this not Jesus, the son of Joseph? Do we not know his father and mother? Then how can he say, 'I have come down from heaven'?" Jesus answered and said to them, "Stop murmuring among yourselves. No one can come to me unless the Father who sent me draw him, and I will raise him on the last day. It is written in the prophets: *They shall all be taught by God.* Everyone who listens to my Father and learns from him comes to me. Not that anyone has seen the Father except the one who is from God; he has seen the Father. Amen, amen, I say to you, whoever believes has eternal life. I am the bread of life. Your ancestors ate the manna in the desert, but they died; this is the bread that comes down from heaven so that one may eat it and not die. I am the living bread that came down from heaven; whoever eats this bread will live forever; and the bread that I will give is my flesh for the life of the world."

Reflecting on the Word

Once again, those listening to Jesus are murmuring among themselves because he said, "I am the bread that came down from heaven." They know him and his family and they think that what he is saying is unbelievable. Jesus is aware of the murmuring and the disbelief, but he continues to preach the Good News. Jesus insists, "I am the bread of life." This bread is not only nourishing, but it is also sustaining and satisfying, and it is available to all. Whoever eats this bread receives eternal life.

•••••• ON THE WAY TO MASS

Think about how going to church nourishes us.

ON THE WAY HOME FROM MASS ••••••

We are fed by God in the Word and by the Eucharist. The assembly also sustains us. How can you participate more fully in the Mass?

Living the Word

Do this art project together: On one sheet of paper, draw a loaf of bread. On another sheet, draw a picture of Jesus. Under each, write a description of how each sustains, nourishes, and satisfies you. Bread (or food) gives us physical nourishment, alleviates our hunger, provides us with energy, and helps us grow healthy. Jesus provides us with spiritual nourishment, helps us live, fills our heart, and helps us love one another. Do we need both bread and Jesus? Which one do we need more?

August 15, 2021

Solemnity of the Assumption of the Blessed Virgin Mary

Hearing the Word

Luke 1:46–55

In the name of the Father, and of the Son, and of the Holy Spirit.

And Mary said:

"My soul proclaims the greatness of the Lord; / my spirit rejoices in God my Savior / for he has looked with favor upon his lowly servant. / From this day all generations will call me blessed: / the Almighty has done great things for me, / and holy is his Name. / He has mercy on those who fear him / in every generation. / He has shown the strength of his arm, / and has scattered the proud in their conceit. / He has cast down the mighty from their thrones, / and has lifted up the lowly. / He has filled the hungry with good things, / and the rich he has sent away empty. / He has come to the help of his servant Israel / for he has remembered his promise of mercy, / the promise he made to our fathers, / to Abraham and his children for ever." /

Reflecting on the Word

Mary meets Elizabeth, shares her great joy, and then praises God, who has done great things for her and blessed her. She directs her prayer to the God who has shown mercy, justly sent away the rich, fed the poor, and lifted the lowly. Finally, she praises God, who has fulfilled his promises to the people of Israel. It is a beautiful song of praise to a just and merciful God, a God who has never abandoned her or God's people.

......ON THE WAY TO MASS

What are we celebrating today? Why is Mary so beloved to us?

ON THE WAY HOME FROM MASS ......

Read the excerpt from today's Gospel aloud to your family. When do you find such joy in God that your soul proclaims and your spirit rejoices?

Living the Word

Create a prayer of praise to God with your children. Follow the structure in Mary's prayer. First, write a few lines of how God makes you feel and declare what God has done for you. Second, praise how God is just: what has God done to show mercy and care for the lowly, poor, and marginalized? Lastly, praise God for all creation. After writing your prayer, say it together as a family each night to remind yourselves what a joy it is to have a God who loves and cares for all of us! (If you are musically inclined, try setting your words to music!)

Twenty-First Sunday in Ordinary Time

Hearing the Word

John 6:60–69

In the name of the Father, and of the Son, and of the Holy Spirit.

Many of Jesus' disciples who were listening said, "This saying is hard; who can accept it?" Since Jesus knew that his disciples were murmuring about this, he said to them, "Does this shock you? What if you were to see the Son of Man ascending to where he was before? It is the spirit that gives life, while the flesh is of no avail. The words I have spoken to you are Spirit and life. But there are some of you who do not believe." Jesus knew from the beginning the ones who would not believe and the one who would betray him. And he said, "For this reason I have told you that no one can come to me unless it is granted him by my Father."

As a result of this, many of his disciples returned to their former way of life and no longer accompanied him. Jesus then said to the Twelve, "Do you also want to leave?" Simon Peter answered him, "Master, to whom shall we go? You have the words of eternal life. We have come to believe and are convinced that you are the Holy One of God."

Reflecting on the Word

Some of Jesus' followers had a hard time with some of Jesus' teachings and decided to leave him and return to their former way of life. We wonder: how can they walk away from Jesus? We know that sometimes it's hard, scary, exhausting, and challenging to follow Jesus and accept his gifts to us. We are all called to build up the Kingdom of God. When discipleship becomes frustrating and discouraging, when it's hard to have faith, when those we know might be leaving the church, or when we feel unwanted, God is still calling us. We can choose to walk away, or we can choose to remain in relationship with him. It is a daily choice, one that we must recommit to on a regular basis.

• • • • • • ON THE WAY TO MASS

Have you ever felt that it was too hard to be a Christian? What changed your mind?

ON THE WAY HOME FROM MASS • • • • • •

If Jesus asked you, "Do you also want to leave?" what would you say?

Living the Word

Why do you believe in Jesus? Together write all the reasons why your family believes in God. Ask the children for their answers especially. Then display the list in your prayer space or somewhere all may be reminded why you believe and trust in God, especially in moments of doubt, confusion, or difficulty.

August 29, 2021

Twenty-Second Sunday in Ordinary Time

Hearing the Word
Mark 7:5–8, 14–15, 21–23

In the name of the Father, and of the Son, and of the Holy Spirit.

The Pharisees and scribes questioned [Jesus], "Why do your disciples not follow the tradition of the elders but instead eat a meal with unclean hands?" He responded, "Well did Isaiah prophesy about you hypocrites, as it is written: / *This people honors me with their lips, / but their hearts are far from me; / in vain do they worship me, / teaching as doctrines human precepts.* / You disregard God's commandment but cling to human tradition."

He summoned the crowd again and said to them, "Hear me, all of you, and understand. Nothing that enters one from outside can defile that person; but the things that come out from within are what defile.

"From within people, from their hearts, come evil thoughts, unchastity, theft, murder, adultery, greed, malice, deceit, licentiousness, envy, blasphemy, arrogance, folly. All these evils come from within and they defile."

Reflecting on the Word

The Pharisees and scribes are trying to catch Jesus in defiance of Jewish customs. But Jesus scolds them and accuses them of disregarding God's commandments and clinging to things that separate them from God. God wants within us a heart that remains close to Jesus, and he wants us to love one another. But humanity is filled with sin, which defiles us and separates us from God. We need to reject what fills our heart with sin and turn our hearts to reflect God's loving presence.

•••••• ON THE WAY TO MASS

Do you sometimes choose to do something that you know is wrong? Why?

ON THE WAY HOME FROM MASS

Think about your answers before you went to Mass. When tempted to do the wrong thing, how can you make the right choice?

Living the Word

Help your children draw a large heart on construction paper or poster board. Inside the heart, write all the things that God wants us to have inside our hearts: love, compassion, forgiveness, joy, and so on. Fill the heart so it almost bursts with these good things! Decorate around the heart using vibrant colors, decorations, ribbons, sequins, and so on. During the week, acknowledge when their hearts are following God in what they say and what they do. Encourage them to keep their hearts full of all God's many gifts!

EVERYDAY FAMILY PRAYERS

The Sign of the Cross

The Sign of the Cross is the first prayer and the last—of each day, and of each Christian life. It is a prayer of the body as well as a prayer of words. When we are presented for Baptism, the community traces this sign on our bodies for the first time. Parents may trace it daily on their children. We learn to trace it daily on ourselves and on those whom we love. When we die, our loved ones will trace this holy sign on us for the last time.

In the name of the Father,

and of the Son,

and of the Holy Spirit. Amen.

The Lord's Prayer

The Lord's Prayer, or the Our Father, is a very important prayer for Christians because Jesus himself taught it to his disciples, who taught it to his Church. Today, we say this prayer as part of Mass, in the Rosary, and in personal prayer. There are seven petitions in the Lord's Prayer. The first three ask for God to be glorified and praised, and the next four ask for God to help take care of our physical and spiritual needs.

Our Father, who art in heaven,

hallowed be thy name;

thy kingdom come,

thy will be done

on earth as it is in heaven.

Give us this day our daily bread,

and forgive us our trespasses,

as we forgive those who trespass against us;

and lead us not into temptation, but deliver us from evil.

The Apostles' Creed

The Apostles' Creed is one of the earliest creeds we have; scholars believe it was written in the second century. The Apostles' Creed is shorter than the Nicene Creed, but it states what we believe about the Father, Son, and Holy Spirit. This prayer is sometimes used at Mass, especially at Masses with children, and is part of the Rosary.

I believe in God,

the Father almighty,

Creator of heaven and earth,

and in Jesus Christ, his only Son, our Lord,

who was conceived by the Holy Spirit,

born of the Virgin Mary,

suffered under Pontius Pilate,

was crucified, died and was buried;

he descended into hell;

and on the third day he rose again from the dead;

he ascended into heaven,

and is seated at the right hand of God the Father almighty;

from there he will come to judge the living and the dead.

I believe in the Holy Spirit,

the holy catholic Church,

the communion of saints,

the forgiveness of sins,

the resurrection of the body,

and life everlasting. Amen.

The Nicene Creed

The Nicene Creed was written at the Council of Nicaea in AD 325, when bishops of the Church gathered together in order to articulate true belief in who Christ is and in his relationship to God the Father. The Nicene Creed was the final document of that Council, written so that all the faithful may know the central teachings of Christianity. We say this prayer at Mass.

I believe in one God,

the Father almighty,

maker of heaven and earth,

of all things visible and invisible.

I believe in one Lord Jesus Christ,

the Only Begotten Son of God,

born of the Father before all ages.

God from God, Light from Light,

true God from true God,

begotten, not made, consubstantial with the Father;

through him all things were made.

For us men and for our salvation

he came down from heaven,

and by the Holy Spirit was incarnate of the Virgin Mary,

and became man.

For our sake he was crucified under Pontius Pilate,
he suffered death and was buried,
and rose again on the third day
in accordance with the Scriptures.
He ascended into heaven
and is seated at the right hand of the Father.
He will come again in glory
to judge the living and the dead
and his kingdom will have no end.

I believe in the Holy Spirit, the Lord, the giver of life,
who proceeds from the Father and the Son,
who with the Father and Son is adored and glorified,
who has spoken through the prophets.

I believe in one holy, catholic, and apostolic Church.
I confess one Baptism for the forgiveness of sins
and I look forward to the resurrection of the dead
and the life of the world to come. Amen.

Glory Be (Doxology)

This is a short prayer that Christians sometimes add to the end of psalms. It is prayed during the Rosary and usually follows the opening verse during the Liturgy of the Hours. It can be prayed at any time during the day.

Glory be to the Father

and to the Son

and to the Holy Spirit,

as it was in the beginning

is now, and ever shall be

world without end. Amen.

Hail Mary

The first two lines of this prayer are the words of the angel Gabriel to Mary, when he announces that she is with child (Luke 1:28). The second two lines are Elizabeth's greeting to Mary (Luke 1:42). The last four lines come to us from deep in history, from where and from whom we do not know. This prayer is part of the Rosary and is often used by Christians for personal prayer.

Hail, Mary, full of grace,

the Lord is with thee.

Blessed art thou among women

and blessed is the fruit of thy womb, Jesus.

Holy Mary, Mother of God,

pray for us sinners,

now and at the hour of our death.

Amen.

Grace before Meals

Families pray before meals in different ways. Some families make up a prayer in their own words, other families sing a prayer, and many families use this traditional formula. Teach your children to say this prayer while signing themselves with the cross.

Bless us, O Lord, and these thy gifts,

which we are about to receive from thy bounty,

through Christ our Lord.

Amen.

Grace after Meals

Teach your children to say this prayer after meals, while signing themselves with the cross. The part in brackets is optional.

We give thee thanks, for all thy benefits,

almighty God, who lives and reigns forever.

[And may the souls of the faithful departed,

through the mercy of God, rest in peace.]

Amen.